FUTURE HOMES

Avi Friedman
With Charles Gregoire

FUTURE HOMES

Sustainable Innovative Designs

CONTENTS

7	**PREFACE**
9	Designing Homes for Changing Times
13	**BUILDING A FUTURE HOME: SUSTAINABLE CONSTRUCTION**
15	Green Materials
33	Affordability
45	Innovative Construction
63	Designing Exteriors
75	Creative Designs
87	**FUTURE GARDENS**
89	Xeriscaped Gardens
99	**INSIDE A FUTURE HOME: SUSTAINABLE INTERIORS**
101	Adaptable Interiors
119	Smart Storage
135	Future Kitchens
149	Energy Efficiency
165	Sustainable Utilities
183	Smart Technology
205	**OUR FUTURE HOMES: SUSTAINABLE COMMUNITIES**
207	Livable Denser Communities
219	Communities on the Move
233	Open Spaces
248	Acknowledgments
249	Contributing Firms
251	Bibliography
254	Project & Photography Details

PREFACE

The way we design and build our houses is changing, fueled by recent shifts in demographics and world markets, along with growing concerns about our impact on the physical environment. This book looks at the architectural trends that have grown out of these shifts—and the ways they can be applied to new and existing housing.

All indications are that people will house themselves differently in the coming decades, regardless of where they live. From a demographic perspective, the make-up of society in many nations is becoming much more diverse. Designs proposed by architects and constructed by builders need to be flexible and consider a wider range of household compositions, ages, and living habits such as work-from-home and multigenerational arrangements.

Economic fluctuations also have taken their toll, affecting world markets as well as the lives of individuals as secure employment becomes less common. In addition, an 'affordability gap' has emerged, where the increase in house prices has surpassed the increase in household income. This has made it highly difficult for first-time homebuyers to purchase a dwelling in most urban centers. Home builders need to offer smaller dwellings that are more adaptable to buyers' space needs and budget.

Sustainability is increasingly important. The need to rethink design and construction practices in line with contemporary environmental constraints has taken center stage in recent years. Sustainable development strives to meet social and economic needs without exhausting the resources of future generations. It requires a reduction of the impact of housing on natural resources, both in materials used and energy expended. The use of net-zero and solar-powered homes, innovative ventilation technologies, green roofs, healthy indoor materials, recycled products, and water-efficient systems have increased in response.

Designers are also exploring new means of housing production, with prefabrication emerging as key to reconciling functional design needs with financial constraints. With new technologies such as 3D printing, new components can be produced at a reduced cost and with an improved appearance. Homebuyers are also paying more attention to well-designed homes and are more likely to choose them. In addition, the need to make homes less costly has initiated creativity in interior concepts where the aim is to make small spaces highly efficient. These changes are bound to affect the ways in which homes and communities will be designed and people will house themselves.

The book begins with an introduction that describes current societal transformations that merit new housing concepts. Each chapter lays out aspects of home design and construction and offers innovative solutions to challenges that are described. Topics include community planning, home design, utilities and systems, production and assembly, sustainable features, energy efficiency and interior design and use. Case studies of recent projects selected from around the world illustrate these innovative trends and ideas.

DESIGNING HOMES
FOR CHANGING TIMES

The 21st century has introduced new challenges that have forced a rethinking about the way we design homes and communities. Broadly speaking these challenges came in three ways: environmental, social, and economic. Also arriving in the new century were technological advances with potential to offer solutions to these challenges. With sustainability as an overarching strategy for future retooling and design of our homes, it's worth taking a look at the new challenges we face and the ways they can be approached by stakeholders such as urban planners, architects, designers, builders, and individuals considering building their own home.

THE ROAD AHEAD

The challenges posed by climate change demand urgent consideration and response. In recent decades, a link has been made between economic development, urban forms, and their environmental implications. Chief among the indexes used to evaluate environmental performance are the measures of carbon and ecological footprints applied to both dwellings and communities.

The negative environmental impacts of urban sprawl and the single-family home development have given rise to a call for 'densification' and the building of denser mixed-use developments. This would also reduce various forms of consumption—including natural resources—and justify investments in public transit.

The individual home itself is an environmental concern. Some organizations have established standards that set strict building codes and efficiency criteria, acting essentially as an accreditation system for projects. As such practices proliferate, the design of energy-efficient and net-zero buildings and neighborhoods are likely to become more common.

In the social realm, significant demographic changes in many parts of the world are expected to affect residential design. In general, demographic composition has become more diverse, and greater design flexibility is needed for groups such as singles and single-parent families that in the past were considered marginal by builders. The number of seniors is expected to rise rapidly in many nations—also known as the 'graying' of a population—and many retirees are likely to trade large, hard-to-maintain homes for smaller units. Some will look for apartments close to shopping hubs or transportation routes. There will be a growing interest in adaptable arrangements that accommodate aging in place, multigenerational homes, and assisted living.

The change of the economic landscape in many nations will have an effect on the residential sector. An affordability gap has emerged, where the rate of increase of house prices has far surpassed the growth of family incomes. This widening gulf in affordability in some regions can be explained by higher land and infrastructure costs, offering another argument for densification and the building of affordable neighborhoods. New economic realities have put the single-family detached home beyond the reach of a growing number of first-time homebuyers, increasing the demand for less expensive, smaller units.

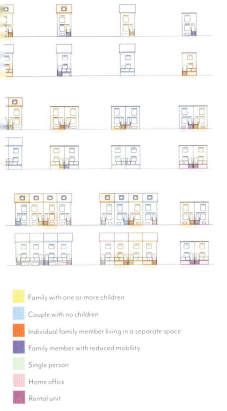

A wide range of housing types in the same project to address demographic diversity

- Family with one or more children
- Couple with no children
- Individual family member living in a separate space
- Family member with reduced mobility
- Single person
- Home office
- Rental unit

9

Transformations are also visible on the technological front. Advancements in technology have provided designers and builders with more efficient mechanisms to design, to construct, and also to reach customers. The digital revolution has had a significant effect on housing design. New methods and technologies allow for simple integration of innovative designs and products contributing to the cost reduction of design and construction, making homes more affordable and cost-efficient.

Among recent innovations, a renewed attention to prefabricated homes has emerged. Future homes may involve a fully automated production where panels are produced using robotic arms for all aspects of fabrication including cutting, nailing, and installing insulation. The next breakthrough in prefabrication may be 3D printing, with the production of physical objects layer by layer using automated computer-controlled machines. The process is still in an incubation stage, but it is being developed rapidly to produce structures with highly complex forms.

Those challenges and responses are likely to define design and construction in years to come. Innovative concepts and practices that are likely to transform the way people will be housed will be further illustrated in the chapters that follow.

CONSIDERING FUTURE GENERATIONS

A review of the social transformations described above raises the question: how should the needed changes be ushered in? How should homes and communities be planned anew or retooled? Sustainability, as a philosophy and organizing principle, has been put forward as an answer to these questions.

The origin of the term *sustainable development* can be traced back several decades. The 1972 United Nations Conference on the Human Environment in Stockholm expressed concerns that humanity was stretching the carrying capacity of the earth to its limits. It was noted that population growth in some nations and overconsumption in others left ecological footprints in the form of land degradation, deforestation, air pollution, and water scarcity. In a 1987 United Nations report called *Our Common Future*, the authors regarded sustainable development as development that met present needs without compromising the ability of future generations to meet their own needs. This definition established a conceptual approach to development, whereby any action taken must be pursued with its future effects in mind. The three pillars of sustainable development that emerged from this document were social, economic, and environmental.

These three pillars of sustainable development provide essential guidance for today's architects and planners—so let's consider each in turn, beginning with social sustainability. The phrase 'social needs' can be interpreted in a multitude of ways, and might be best understood by way of example. For instance, when the creation of a sustainable healthcare system is an objective, ensuring that sufficient funds will continue to be available is essential. A contribution to public health can be achieved by encouraging fitness, as it has been shown that people with an active lifestyle are less likely to suffer from cardiovascular- and diabetes-related

Urban aspects of sustainable communities

ECONOMY

Live/Work

ENVIRONMENT

Rainwater recycling

Mixed-income communities

Orientation for passive solar gain

Multiple services

Recycled content in construction

CULTURE

Nearby schools

SOCIAL

Access to nearby recreational areas

Backyards and gardens

Local food production

Street furniture/ public art

Access to municipal and public spaces

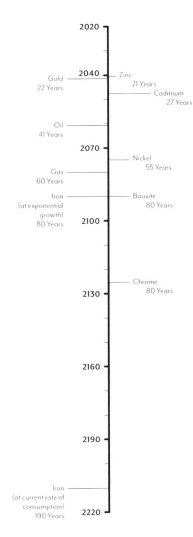

Projected period of availability of natural resources after 2020

illnesses. It is, therefore, in the best interest of municipalities that neighborhoods are designed with bicycle and pedestrian pathways.

Cultural sustainability is equally vital. Promoting vernacular culture and preserving local traditions contributes to society in both direct and indirect ways. Most obviously, old buildings are visible reminders of human history, giving us a direct connection to the past. More indirectly, heritage inspires young architects and planners, thus improving the quality of future buildings and designs.

We cannot afford to ignore economic sustainability. Bad planning decisions today burden the generations of tomorrow. Building excessively wide roads, for example, will have long-term economic effects. Such streets will need to be resurfaced periodically, and in cold climates more snow will accumulate, requiring more funding for its removal. When a development is privately initiated, the cost of wider roads will raise the price of each house. This forces buyers to borrow more money that they will then be forced to repay over a longer period, thereby putting at risk their own financial sustainability.

Environmental sustainability is concerned with ecological attributes created by the construction and upkeep of a development, including its roads, open spaces, and homes. An assessment tool of how a development will protect existing ecosystems is necessary for planners. This is in regard not only to the initial effect of choice of materials, for example, but also their long-term performance and recyclability. Asphalt-covered roads will make rainwater runoff stream to manholes, for example, while creating bioswales (channels or trenches) at the side of roads will promote the growth of rainwater flora when it is planted, thereby saving runoff.

These pillars critical to sustainable development can be viewed independently, as discussed in this chapter. Yet, when one closely examines dwellings and neighborhoods that are designed and built on sound sustainable principles, it is evident that these aspects are critically interrelated.

DESIGNING HOMES FOR CHANGING TIMES

BUILDING A FUTURE HOME:
SUSTAINABLE CONSTRUCTION

Sustainable materials and methods are changing the way we build new homes. Anyone designing or building a sustainable home needs to choose what they build from and how they go about it, as well as considering costs, both financially and in terms of energy expended in the building process.

If you use the right building materials it increases the lifetime of the home, but it's also important to consider the impact of your materials on the environment at every stage of the process, from the way they are harvested all the way through to what happens when the building is dismantled.

Affordability is a key aspect of sustainability. Efficient use of materials, simplified construction methods, and use of increasingly impressive prefabrication and 3D printing technology are all ways to reduce costs as well as environmental impacts.

This section examines building materials and how to evaluate their sustainability; affordable options are discussed, and innovations in prefabrication are outlined. Floor plans, exterior and façade designs, and construction methods are all considered. And some inspirational examples of sustainable homes will provide some ideas for anyone starting out on their future-home journey.

GREEN MATERIALS

What are the most sustainable materials builders and designers can choose for future homes? Building materials need to be selected carefully, since poor choices may adversely affect their surroundings over their lifetime, and it's worthwhile to consider the impact of building materials on the environment all the way from their harvesting through to the dismantling of the building. This chapter look at ways to evaluate the sustainability of materials and discusses a few of the most environmentally responsible options available.

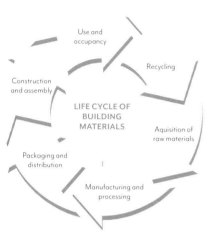

A sustainable life cycle of building materials

Building materials are usually classified as either naturally occurring or engineered. 'Naturally occurring' includes organic materials such as wood, bamboo, and straw, as well as minerals and rocks such as metal ores, stone, and earth. Engineered products are derived from natural resources through physical, mechanical, or chemical processing and include cement and synthetics such as plastics and paints. Less wasteful use of naturally occurring products, or engineered products more sensitive to the environment, need to be the objective of any design and construction process.

When selecting sustainable building materials, it helps to make a life-cycle assessment from manufacturing through disposal. The main aspects to consider are contribution to climate change, fossil fuel depletion, transportation, toxic effects on humans, eco-toxicity, waste disposal, and water extraction. This analysis is also referred to as a cradle-to-grave assessment; environmentalists advocate for this kind of assessment, which promotes the reuse and recycling of products instead of their disposal. This brings the process full circle in a closed loop that conserves energy and virgin resources, and minimizes waste. The process involves six major phases: acquisition of raw materials, processing and manufacturing, packaging and distribution, construction and assembly, use and occupancy, and, finally, recycling or disposal.

CHOOSING GREEN MATERIALS AND PRODUCTS

Architects and builders can influence the sustainability of a manufacturing process by specifying which building materials will be used. When you choose products that have ISO 14000/14001 environmental labels, for example, this encourages demand for—and supply of—products that stress the environment the least. It's always best to choose materials that consume less energy and minimize waste disposal by recycling or reusing waste generated at source or by manufacturers.

The most sustainable products use natural local resources or recycled ingredients in place of virgin ones, recycle any waste generated by its processes, have low embodied energy, are biodegradable, have minimal derivation from petrochemicals, and are designed for reuse and recyclability. Ideally, these products are also nontoxic, nonhazardous, recyclable or reusable, locally obtained, and energy and water efficient, and their manufacturing, occupancy, and demolition are environmentally responsible.

DID YOU KNOW?

→ Insulated Concrete Forms (ICFs) are forms that are left in place after the concrete is poured for a foundation or wall. The forms are generally made of foam insulation, such as expanded polystyrene (EPS), and are filled with reinforced concrete to create a solid structure. Sustainable benefits from ICF systems are: optimized energy performance, durability, recycled material content, local materials, and improved indoor air quality.

→ Structural Insulated Panels (SIPs) are panels with a core of rigid foam insulation between an exterior and interior skin. Panels are custom designed, prefabricated, and assembled on site, which reduces waste, construction time, and labor costs. Their solid structure allows air tightness with high thermal insulation and minimal levels of air infiltration. In addition, this integrated system uses less wood than a conventional wood frame house.

→ Engineered wood is a sustainable alternative to traditional wood siding or joists. It's made of wood fibers combined with bonding agents that create a composite lightweight product with superior strength. Use of engineered boards for flooring and roof sheathing instead of common plywood can lead to savings in embodied energy.

FUTURE HOME FEATURES:

DE GOUVERNEUR

→ **Sustainable and recycled building materials**
→ **Affordable materials**
→ **Natural light and ventilation**

Second-floor plan

Third-floor plan

Ground-floor plan

First-floor plan

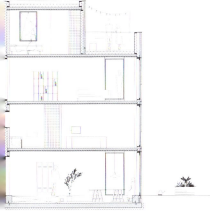
Section

The cityscape of Rotterdam in the Netherlands is dense, yet one can spot many empty plots as a result of post-war town planning that distinguished between old and new buildings. These gaps now become desired sites for infill projects, such as **De Gouverneur**, which was designed by the architects at Studio Architectuur MAKEN for themselves in 2016. During the design process they limited the house's impact on the neighboring buildings and on the environment.

The four-story-tall house is separated from its neighbor on one side by a narrow strip of land, maintaining the passage to the backyard. This path also helps a side window to let in enough natural light and on the other side, it shares a wall with the neighboring building. Each floor of the house is dedicated to one function, that become more private toward the top. The ground floor contains an open kitchen and dining area, connecting to a backyard garden. On the first floor, office space takes up much of the area. The living space is on the third, and the top floor is reserved for the bedroom and a rooftop terrace. The street façade has two openings, while the rear is punctured with many large openings to let sunlight in.

The architects opted to use brick to blend in with the façades of the street's other buildings. Sustainability however was an issue, since regular brick consumes a high amount of embodied carbon. To resolve this problem, they collaborated with StoneCycling, a startup that used construction rubble to created recycled materials. Waste from construction accounts for 65 percent of all waste in the Netherlands; most of this is exported for disposal, or downcycled for use in paving roads where their value decreases drastically. StoneCycling retains the value of these materials by upcycling them into bricks for new construction, creating a circular economy. Emissions in transportation are kept to a minimum as well, sourcing bricks from within a 62-mile (100-kilometer) radius. Using slices of the brick that show the rubble results in a pleasing color variation. The brick color scheme fits in with existing buildings, combined with a subtle relief pattern at the top of the façade.

The architects took a risk in using StoneCycling bricks, since this house was the first project to incorporate the product. The result is a modern home that is contextually sensitive, showing that sustainability does not need to be sacrificed for style.

GREEN MATERIALS

GREEN MATERIALS

FUTURE HOME FEATURES:
TK-33

→ Sustainable building materials
→ Affordable construction costs
→ Adaptable interiors
→ Natural heating

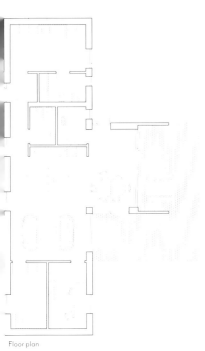
Floor plan

Identifying materials that would help cut the carbon footprint of the construction process was the first step for the architects of **TK-33**, a rural home north of Copenhagen designed for a senior couple by Danish firm Tegnestuen LOKAL in 2017.

In a typical Danish home, concrete and brick are the primary materials. But concrete is a large contributor to CO_2 emissions due to the production process of cement, and brick also makes a sizable impact during its production and because of its low reusability.

In the design of TK-33, the load-bearing structure typically made of concrete was replaced by timber framing, using a material that is both renewable and has lower emissions in the extraction and manufacturing stages. A thin layer of brick shingles was used to envelope the façades and its reusability was ensured by its consumer-to-consumer (C2C) certification, in case replacements need to be made. The brick cladding is high in durability, increasing the lifespan of the wooden framing underneath and decreasing the emissions impact.

Sustainability considerations went beyond the materials used in the project. The home has a T-shaped plan, with the main social areas occupying the center. The flexible space includes a living area, open kitchen, and dining area, which are all connected to an L-shaped, south-facing deck. The omission of walls allows this space to be rearranged to accommodate future owners as well. Expansive, floor-to-ceiling glazing on the central wall takes full advantage of the southwest sun. Private spaces are located to the two sides of the central atrium. One end is the master suite, which opens to its own terrace; the other end contains a guest room and an office. All installations are gathered in a central service core that borders the kitchen and encompasses two bathrooms and the laundry room. By reducing the distance between different utility functions, construction costs are cut down.

The project practices sustainability through its careful selection of materials, cutting down the carbon footprint of the construction process while providing a unique material identity for the house. Despite limitations in material choice, the project embodies a comfortable, ideal style of modern living that showcases the feasibility of sustainable design.

Though a variety of sustainable and environmentally conscious building materials like those used in De Gouverneur and TK-33 have become available, they are not always selected by designers for new construction projects. This may be due to differences in price, or lack of awareness of newer products. More often than not, designers overlook the use of environmentally conscious building products due to cost, failing to realize that maintenance and future costs will be reduced. The products listed on p16 are ideal for the construction process of environmentally responsible dwellings; architects and designers have the opportunity to make buildings more sustainable by specifying the use of such products.

AFFORDABILITY

Increased density means more homes on the site and a lower cost of land for each dwelling

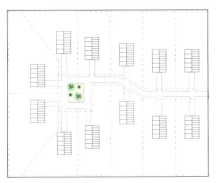

2 dwellings / acre (2 dwellings / 0.4 hectare net)
12 dwelling units
6 acres (2.4 developed hectares)

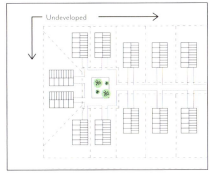

2 dwellings / acre (4 dwellings / 0.4 hectare net)
12 dwelling units
3 acres (1.2 developed hectares)

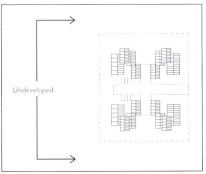

8 dwellings / acre (8 dwellings / 0.4 hectare net)
12 dwelling units
1.5 acres (0.6 developed hectares)

In an affordable housing project, the costs of land, infrastructure, and construction, among others, need to be reduced without compromising comfort and livability. It's possible to lower the cost of a dwelling through efficient use of material and non-material resources by simplifying the building complexity. This chapter lists design strategies that when followed can lower construction costs.

HEIGHT AND DENSITY

The number of floors and the building's height is subject to zoning by laws and will affect the project's cost. While the height will have the greatest impact on land-use efficiency and housing density, it can also substantially affect the use of building materials, and, to some extent, energy efficiency and overall cost. Vertical designs make most efficient use of space, since more stacking results in the need for less construction material. The cost of a two-story square house, for instance, is lower than a one-story with equivalent area, since it has half the foundation and roof area.

The form of the envelope's surface is another aspect worth considering. When a building has several projections—the upper floor extends beyond the lower, for example—costs are bound to rise. Projections, therefore, need to be introduced where they are most needed. Providing a cover above an entry door or creating a suspended bay are functional uses for a projection. One also needs to bear in mind that the floor of a projected area must be well insulated to prevent infiltration of cold air in wintertime.

When the density increases, the cost per unit declines. Attaching units to each other, therefore, can make them more affordable. When considering methods and forms of attachment, the designers need to pay attention to the project's budget, appearance, and livability. They need to place the units next to each other in a way that makes the occupants feel that they reside in a lower-density setting. Placing the unit close to the street will save on the cost of extension of utilities. The method of connecting the utilities to each unit will depend on the legal title of the project. When the project is sold as a *condominium*, only one connection will be needed from the main utility source to a block of units. When the project is sold as *freehold*, separate connections will have to be made to each unit, thereby increasing the cost.

Building homes in a row lowers the cost. The main advantage is savings on land and infrastructure costs. Simply put, the more units are joined together, the greater the savings will be. Joining the units results in a 33 percent savings in lot area and street length, and 70 percent savings in the exterior wall perimeter. Joining between four and eight units no wider than 20 feet (6 meters) each is recommended.

The use of local traditional building methods and fewer advanced technologies can also bring the cost down. Building processes that have been used with proven positive outcomes are commonly preferable to those that employ expensive technologies. Passive heating and ventilation, for example, will offer better results and cost less.

TOP TO BOTTOM:
ROOFS AND BASEMENTS

When designing a basement, careful planning can result in lowering construction costs and having a more livable space. A key question will be how to use a basement. A large home will permit the fitting of both living and service functions on upper levels. In a small, affordable home, choices will be limited. Recent improvements in construction technology have contributed to making the basement a livable space and an independent accessory unit. The unit may have its own entrance and can be used as a source of supplementary income for the household, which might reside above.

Designing to use roof space efficiently can also cut costs. In a lower-cost dwelling, a flat roof can provide an area for future expansion. The design must ensure that the existing structure will support another floor, which would be easily accessed. When pitched roofs are designed, attention should be given to their complexity. Intricate roofs will not only take more time to assemble, but when poorly constructed can become a source of heat loss.

FUTURE HOME FEATURES:
EXPANDABLE HOUSE

→ **Densification**
→ **Affordability**
→ **Recycling and energy efficiency**
→ **Local materials**
→ **Flexibility**

AFFORDABLE HOMES

As times change and technology advances, all the tools are out there to help us make the lives of homebuyers easier and keep costs lower. With the development of specialized software, a person interested in buying a house can access and select from all the catalogs, the type of unit (single, duplex, triplex), location, attachment from other units (detached, semi-detached, row-house), materials and colors of the façades, internal layout, and additional components (storage, kitchen configuration and so on) of their ideal house.

Flexibility and affordability are the main focus of **Expandable House**, designed specifically in 2019 for the town of Batam, Indonesia, by Urban Rural Systems, a team at Future Cities Laboratory whose research and development focuses on solutions for growing cities. In the past half century, Batam increased in size and population from a small fishing village to a city of one million people—and growing. This raised issues of how to house the large numbers of incoming migrants, organize sewage systems, and provide transportation infrastructure. Expandable House tackles the housing problem through a flexible structure that can adapt to the homeowner's needs.

Since every household differs in their needs, Expandable House is customizable to fulfill them. The Urban Rural Systems team studied patterns of household income generation, as well as the consumption of water, energy, and food, to develop a spatial layout that can flexibly and affordably meet these requirements. The most basic form of the house consists of a one-story, open-plan layout. The height of the roof can be raised; the dwelling's floor and foundations are structurally capable of supporting up to three additional floors, which would be added in between the foundation and the roof. The developer can sell the basic model of the house, allowing the homeowner to add infill levels according to their needs or their budget. They may also choose to use the home as a live/work unit by allocating the ground floor for commercial functions, generating income that can in turn pay for the house. This form of housing curbs urban sprawl by encouraging densifying vertically instead. The basic model is inexpensive to construct, using local brick for walls and corrugated steel for the roof. Due to the adaptable nature of the house, it prevents unnecessary elements from being built, further cutting down costs.

Although the structure of the house is very minimal, it comes with all resources needed to live sustainably, including rainwater harvesting, solar power generation, and sewage/septic-tank systems. The house is also designed using passive cooling principles to avoid reliance on centralized energy infrastructure that is costly to build and disturbs the environment. A kitchen garden is included as an integral part of the house, encouraging self-sufficiency as part of the residents' lifestyles.

Expandable House is affordable yet can be flexibly adapted to each homeowner's needs. Although it was proposed as a social housing solution, its ability to be self-sufficient and sustainable surpasses that of many market-rate homes. Another space-saving (and as a result cost-saving) strategy is to make the interior highly efficient by better planning the circulation.

Another type of dwelling designed to keep costs down and adapt to the local context is **Mausam—House of the Seasons**, designed and built by Zero Studio in Mannarkand, India, in 2017. In today's India, architecture can be seen as a status symbol. Upper-class citizens can own professionally designed homes with air conditioning and various technologies, while other citizens who cannot afford these luxuries live in smaller replicas of these houses, which do not offer the same comfort. It is easy for architecture to lose its focus, forgetting traditional techniques that offer shelter from the climate. Zero Studio designed Mausam—House of the Seasons with the intention of reviving vernacular customs of home building, to show that a well-made house does not need to follow a certain aesthetic or become costly to construct.

This family home for a retired army officer and his wife was designed on three split levels, following the sloping site. Common spaces are expandable, to accommodate visits by their four daughters. While the bedrooms are located on the ground floor, a variety of living areas and balconies connect to the central staircase to give different views and settings.

Without temperature control through mechanical systems, the house relies on passive design principles instead to maintain a comfortable temperature inside. Many openings of the house are covered with brick jalis—ornamental latticed screens—rather than glass. This promotes air circulation inside and produces better natural ventilation, while providing an interesting interplay of light and shadow throughout the day. The steep roofs make up a large portion of the façade, each with a substantial overhang that prevents harsh summer sunlight from entering. The terracotta roof tiles absorb exterior heat but do not transfer it indoors.

The tiles were sourced from a demolished house near the site; all other materials used in the construction were also local. The walls are comprised of laterite brick with a plaster finish, flooring is made of terracotta, and there are interior finishes of timber. The interiors are kept minimal, cutting down costs. The architects enlisted help from local workers to build this house. Native plants and trees were grown around the house to better situate it in its site, creating a different look for the home as the seasons change.

The architects were able to achieve a sensitively designed house that is fitting for its context. Without a large budget, the home is still a comfortable place for the couple to spend their retirement.

FUTURE HOME FEATURES:

MAUSAM—HOUSE OF THE SEASONS

→ Recycled and local materials
→ Affordable materials
→ Natural ventilation and cooling
→ Vernacular building methods

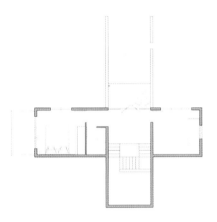

First-floor plan

Ground-floor plan

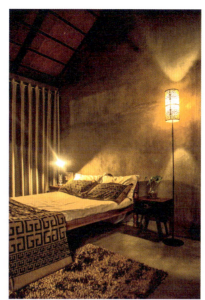

AFFORDABILITY

INNOVATIVE CONSTRUCTION

Modular and panelized prefabricated types

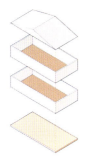

Modular

Panelized

Prefabrication has come of age as digital and fabrication technology advances, such as 3D printing, have renewed designers' interest in factory-built housing. Contemporary prefabricated homes have shed the past stigma that regarded them as monotonous and technically inferior to conventionally constructed units. In Japan, for example, one third of all newly built homes are made in a factory. If you were to point a finger at a technology that is likely to transform the building industry, prefabrication is the one, with innovations continuing to emerge.

WHY GO PREFAB?

The rising trend in prefabricated homes can be attributed to their financial, environmental, structural, and time-saving advantages. In addition, constructing houses in a factory negates problems such as vandalism, material storage, and weather delays. Factories also require fewer skilled workers and therefore the end product becomes cheaper. An efficient, high-tech factory can produce a house in a week, as compared to on-site construction which, on average, takes more than five months.

As is the case with any manufactured component, waste generated by prefabrication of panel systems is less than what could be expected from on-site construction. Considering that the construction of an average house produces some 5,512 pounds (2.5 tons) of waste—25 percent of which is dimensional lumber and an additional 15 percent is manufactured wood products—cost savings can be substantial, particularly in large developments.

There are several types of prefabricated systems, subsystems, and components that can be combined at various levels to provide a complete system package. 'Modular construction' refers to factory fabrication of sections that can consist of an entire house or part of one. The sections are sent to the site where they are hoisted into place by crane. 'Kits of parts' consists of well-marked building products, such as studs or windows, that are shipped to the site for assembly. 'Panelization,' the most widely used, is the third method. Panels of different sizes, some with framing only and others with insulation and windows, are assembled according to plans.

One of the most significant advantages of prefabricated panel systems is the superior quality that can be achieved through the manufacturing process. This quality can be evaluated based on the interrelated characteristics of craftsmanship, technical performance, and durability.

WHICH PANELS?

Panel systems that are applicable to wood-frame residential construction can be divided into three categories:

→ open-sheathed panels
(using conventional construction methods)

→ structural sandwich panels

→ unsheathed structural panels

For each of the systems, it is possible to 'add value' to the panel by integrating a larger portion of the building envelope during fabrication. Added components vary from air barriers to exterior and/or interior finishes. The extent to which the panels are finished has different implications for the builder and the worker who will select and install the system.

Unsheathed structural panels appear to provide good performance in all respects but benefit from few extraordinary characteristics. The biggest advantage is that they can overcome the inadequate workmanship that may be found in conventional construction without resorting to very unfamiliar building techniques. The use of expanded polystyrene foam between the structural elements significantly improves the performance of the wall in that area, which is a key failure point in conventionally built walls: discontinuous insulation and air barrier caused by improper installation.

FUTURE HOME FEATURES:
FAB HOUSE

→ **Prefabricated elements**
→ **Natural light and ventilation**
→ **Affordable materials**
→ **Metal cladding**

FAB House, a large-scale project in the UK, is an example of dwellings constructed mainly off-site using prefabricated frames and panels. Designed by TDO and architect George Clarke in 2018, it's a 10-unit town-house project in North Shields, in the northeast of England. It was commissioned by joint venture developers Urban Splash and Places for People in a masterplan to revitalize Smith's Dock, a former shipyard, into an urban neighborhood that included two rows of five town-house units. The town houses adopt an open floor plan for the living spaces on the first floor. The entryway is adjoined by the kitchen, which leads to the dining area, then a large living area toward the back of the house. The exposed ceiling joists detail is especially noticeable here, where it raises ceiling heights to 9.5 feet (2.9 meters) and works in conjunction with the open plan to provide a more spacious feeling to the home. At the same time, it adds character to the space by showcasing the materiality of the timber joists, which becomes part of a cohesive material scheme along with the birch-faced plywood staircase.

The stairwell is lit by a large skylight running lengthwise, and floor-to-ceiling windows can be found in the reception space and the master bedroom. The large amount of natural light flooding into the interior makes rooms appear larger, especially on the second floor where the space is sectioned off into two main bedrooms and one child's bedroom. For the exterior of the town houses, TDO references the site's industrial heritage through the materiality of the façades, by using a dark gray Equitone panel cladding combined with shrouds of COR-TEN steel.

The modules of FAB House were fabricated in a facility off-site, in collaboration with manufacturer SIG. Each unit has dimensions of 16.5 feet (5 meters) width and 36 feet (11 meters) depth in accordance with size restrictions for transportation of the modules. The design of the cladding system features a central alignment to facilitate assembly for the contractors, who would only need to align two instead of four; the central alignment is also present in windows and doors. The cladding conceals a zone for services, which are connected externally on site.

FAB House is an innovative development into the applications of prefabrication in architecture for affordable housing on a larger scale; specifically, in how it can be used to increase efficiency in production but maintain the spatial and living qualities of a more traditionally designed home.

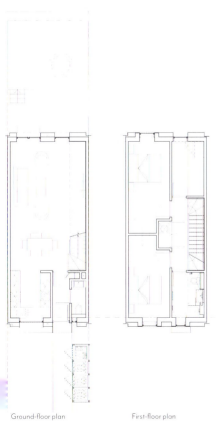

Ground-floor plan   First-floor plan

INNOVATIVE CONSTRUCTION

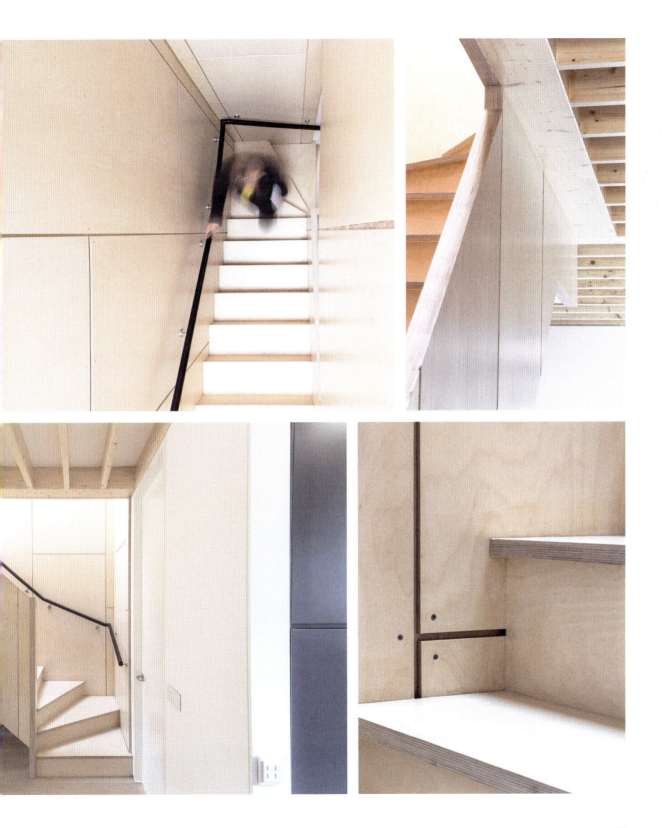

INNOVATIVE CONSTRUCTION

FUTURE HOME FEATURES:
SYSHAUS

→ Prefabricated elements
→ Customizable layout
→ Recyclable materials
→ Smart-home technologies

Floor plan

Another prefabricated construction is **SysHaus**, a one-story eco-friendly house designed in 2018 in São Paulo, Brazil, by architect Arthur Casas for the engineering and construction startup company SysHaus. The company aims to produce prefabricated homes that provide customers with transparency in terms of costs, with a six-month timeline from design to construction completion and assembly lasting 28 days, and with a 20-year warranty.

The house has a large, linear open-plan living area connected to the dining area and kitchen. Storage and cabinets in the kitchen space were designed as independent modules that can be removed and easily installed again. They also allow the layout to be rearranged to the inhabitants' liking, as the island is also moveable. An outdoor living area, much like an engawa—the strip of decking between the house and garden in Japanese architecture—creates a harmonious relation between the interior and the house's surroundings. In the prototypal unit built in São Paulo, it highlights the landscaping done by Renata Tilli, who selected plants that are adaptable to various climates.

The structural system of the home was developed by SysHaus and include same-section pillars and beams connected by structural nodes. This system provides possibilities for different spatial configurations, with a height limit of three floors, on flat or sloped terrain. The interior finishes, including flooring and walls, were designed as a docking system. Altogether, this ensures that the construction and disassembly processes do not generate any waste or require natural resources.

All materials used in the construction of the house are recyclable. There is an option to add a green roof to the bungalow. Other sustainability features include a rainwater collection system, and photovoltaic cells to harvest solar energy, as well as a biodigestor that converts waste into gas for use in the kitchen or for heating. SysHaus also makes use of new smart-home technologies, with options to install smart locks, security cameras for added security, and a water management system all controlled by mobile phone.

The design pushes the boundaries of creating a sustainable home. The adaptability of the structural system is combined with the flexibility of the interior storage spaces and home automation features to form a modern home that can be customized.

3D PRINTING AND FULLY AUTOMATED PRODUCTION

Recent advances mean that 3D printing promises to be the next breakthrough in prefabrication. In general, it is the production of physical objects layer by layer, using automated computer-controlled machines. The most common types of printers are gantry-type systems that were developed for additive manufacturing, where materials like cement keep being added to build a structure. Other methods include cable-suspended printing heads and small robots. The chosen method commonly depends on the material used. The process is still in an incubation stage, but it is being developed rapidly to produce structures with highly complex forms. Some of the most notable examples are homes built entirely out of cement that is added in place and wooden partitions constructed using robotic arms.

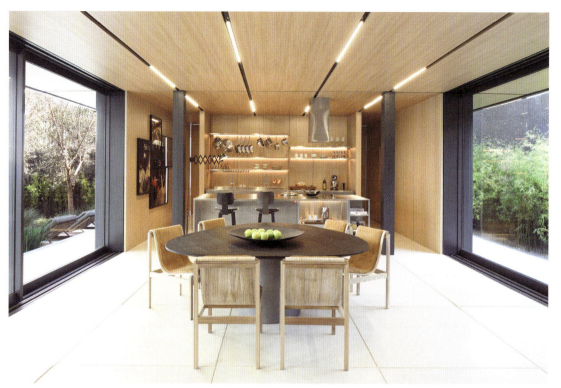

DESIGNING EXTERIORS

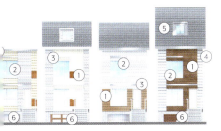

Features that contribute to the diversity of façades in multi-unit projects

1 Materials/cladding
2 Window sizes
3 Sunbreaks
4 Roof shapes
5 Roof shingles
6 Garages

Allowing buyers to personalize the home's exterior is likely to be the way of the future as more people will live in high-density urban settings. The goal is to create a mass-customized community where the dwellings have common underlying exterior design principles but where people also have the opportunity to make their own imprint on the façade.

MATERIALS AND METHODS

Dwellings can be constructed in a variety of configurations. Detached or semi-detached homes give the designer a greater envelope area to work with. The elevations also account for the building's energy performance. More windows mean more places for the heat in winter or cold air in summer to escape through. The choice between transparent and opaque, therefore, needs to be carefully made, considering the orientation and interior design.

Window Choices

Heat losses throughout a building can occur by any of the following three processes: conduction, convection, and radiation. And in all three cases, windows are the weakest link and, as such, represent the most important investment in the construction or renovation of any dwelling. They are also highly variable in price, appearance, and performance, making their selection a difficult process.

Generally, windows with fewer operable parts are less costly and more energy efficient. The longer the joint, the greater the potential for heat loss through leakage; therefore, fixed windows are best in this regard. As for operable windows, pivoting components are more energy efficient, since they make use of compression seals. Sliding parts are least effective in terms of air leakage.

Construction practices have changed in recent years and they keep doing so. Innovation has brought new sustainable building products that reduce consumption of natural resources as well as saving money for builders and buyers. Some of these products have gained acceptance and are widely used in exteriors, while others have encountered resistance.

The two main new products are engineered lumber and light-gauge steel. These manufactured products are used as joists, beams, and flooring materials.

Glue-laminated lumber is stacked, finger-jointed layers of standard lumber. Another similar product is laminated-veneer lumber, which is made from thin layers of wood that have been glued together and run parallel to each other.

CREATIVE FAÇADES

Several strategies have been used to counteract monotony when the dwellings are attached, with solutions ranging from simple to complex. The easiest way to add character visually is through the choice of façade materials. Brick, for example, a material with timeless quality, comes in many patterns and colors. Wood siding is another vernacular option that, when painted in different shades, can produce a colorful setting.

In a large project, the architect can offer a choice of façade features. For example, buyers may choose to have a front door with a porch, a balcony on the second floor, and a gabled roof. Their neighbors may choose to have a bay window on the first floor, two windows with no balcony on the second, and a flat roof. This mass-customization method not only creates more diverse and interesting neighborhoods, but it also enhances the occupants' sense of personalization.

A creative façade system is the highlight of **Đại Kim House** in Hanoi, Vietnam. Built in 2018 by Aline Architect, it was designed to maximise natural ventilation while retaining visual interest.

Houses in Vietnam commonly follow a town-house typology and share a wall with one another, each occupying a narrow and long plot of land. The humid, tropical climate makes natural ventilation a main design focus. Đại Kim House tackles this issue in its façade, which uses multiple different material layers to filter air and light entering the home.

The façade is made up of three layers; the outermost wall is mostly opaque, punctured with openings of various shapes and sizes, corresponding to the programs located on each floor. These are filled with patterned metal grids that offer the house privacy from the street, and at the same time create visual interest for both sides. This layer prevents harsh, direct sunlight from reaching the interiors; the patterned metal acts as a delicate brise-soleil. Behind the wall is a void reserved for greenery. On the balcony of every floor, plants and trees are placed to shape a buffer from dust in the streets and in the air. These also bring nature closer to the interior. Fully glazed glass doors further blur the boundary between inside and outside. The glass visually connects the two spaces, while blocking much of the excessive heat to maintain a comfortable temperature inside.

The functions of the house are organized on split levels around a staircase in the center of the house. The stairwell is open air, acting as a large light well that more easily lets light into all corners of the home. This also facilitates natural ventilation, providing an abundance of fresh air to enter all spaces. Due to the split levels, distances between rooms are reduced, resulting in a more connected spatial flow throughout. Stair landings become a buffer space, increasing efficiency in space by eliminating the need for hallways.

The multilayer façade treatment of Đại Kim House deals with the tropical climate in a way that maximizes ventilation and views while maintaining comfort. It allows the homeowners to enjoy living immersed in nature while in an urban environment.

FUTURE HOME FEATURES:
ĐẠI KIM HOUSE

→ Innovative façade
→ Natural ventilation
→ Visual interest
→ Green spaces

Second-floor plan

Third-floor plan

Ground-floor plan

First-floor plan

FUTURE HOME FEATURES:
DOUBLE DUPLEX

- → Innovative façade
- → Natural heating and ventilation
- → Increases density
- → Creative repurposing of traditional styles

Upper unit second level

Upper unit first level

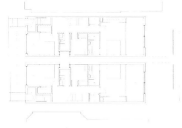

Lower unit second level

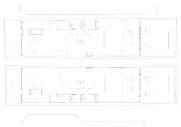

Lower unit first level

CHOOSING A ROOF

Much of a house's façade appearance is determined by the roof. Gabled roofs are one option; however, if the roof is pitched in the narrow dimension and built in a row, in cold climate zones there will be snow accumulation between units, making this configuration unsuitable in Nordic climates. A roof that slopes down toward the front and rear will be appropriate for any climate. A shed roof is another possibility, which allows for alternation of direction among houses in rows, creating a more interesting streetscape. Depending on which type of roof is chosen, a variety of architectural details can be incorporated to enhance the dwelling's curb appeal.

Steep roofs on tall buildings that mimic the older houses around them—in addition to a creative façade—are a feature of **Double Duplex**, two houses built by Batay-Csorba Architects in Toronto, Canada, in 2015. Double Duplex fits in with the local context yet stands out in its historic neighborhood, among the older Victorian bay and gable styles of Toronto's Parkdale district.

Batay-Csorba Architects identified a lack of diverse housing types in the city's urban core—there are many apartment and condo developments, but none that densify older residential neighborhoods. With Double Duplex, they aimed to develop an infill project that doubles the occupancy of the site, dividing each building into two dwellings stacked on top of one another.

The two houses were created upon the bay and gable typology. A typical home of this historic style consists of large windows on the street façade, steep roofs, a strong verticality produced by the narrow constraints of the sites, and often a front balcony. Double Duplex retains all of these characteristics, establishing a formal connection with the neighbors. It also incorporates an element of ornamental motif common in older 19th-century homes.

Batay-Csorba designed an intricate street-facing brise-soleil that mimics the craft of older houses, reinterpreting it for the modern context to engage the movement of passers-by. The façade contains fragments placed at various angles, giving different effects throughout the day as the light highlights different surfaces. The brise-soleil was created much like an art installation. As people walk by, figures appear and disappear, reminiscent of cloud animals; the piece embodies visibility without space. For the residents of these units, the dynamic façade filters light into the homes in a textured way, providing visual interest. At night the brise-soleil functions much like a lantern cover for the light from inside the homes.

The large windows referenced from bay and gable houses benefit the lower unit; the architects implemented a double-height space in the front to exploit the light. The back of the unit leads to a sunken courtyard, further blurring the boundary between ground level and basement. The upper unit has an abundance of outdoor space, with a double-height balcony concealed by the brise-soleil façade as well as a master bedroom terrace on the top floor. The interior ceiling joists are exposed, featuring blocking in a pattern mirroring that of the façade.

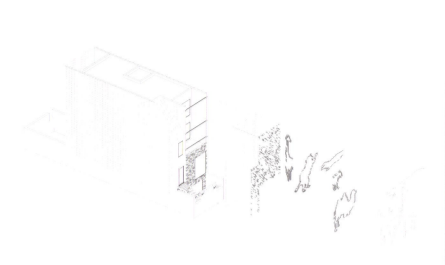

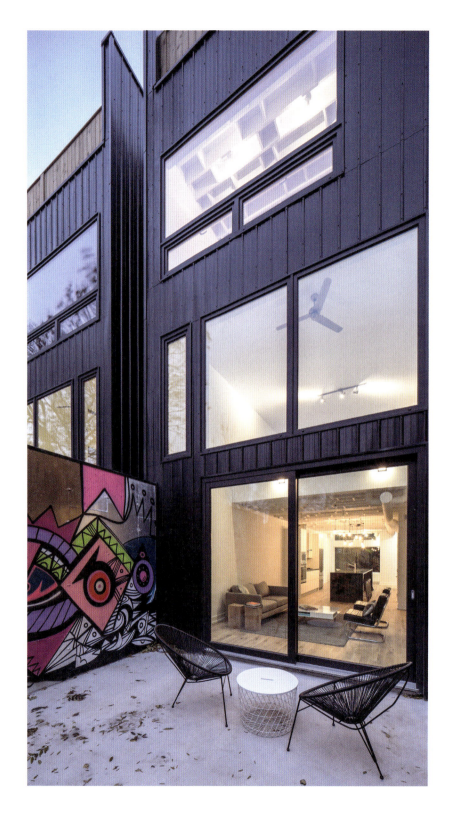

DESIGNING EXTERIORS

CREATIVE DESIGNS

Design aspects of narrow dwellings

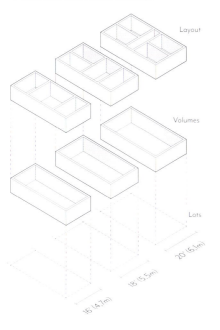

Relation between dwelling and the ground

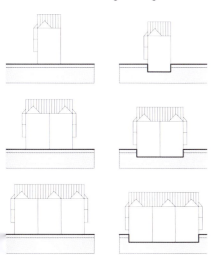

Designing future homes will pose several challenges. Homes will have to be functional and address new lifestyle trends, be comfortable to live in, be affordable and energy efficient, and be sustainable in their construction and operation. This seems to be a tall order from a designer, builder, and homebuyer. Yet, it offers opportunities to be creative and address issues that in the past were considered marginal. It's worth looking at the broader design process to see what paths are available to creating a future home.

Square or Rectangle?

With the need to make homes adaptable to a wide range of occupants, the conceptual approach should be to aim to make any space look larger. Commonly, the proportions of the dwelling's footprint can be either square or rectangular. The interior of a home with a square plan is likely to be easier to subdivide. When the unit is detached, there will also be greater flexibility in the placement of windows. The disadvantage of a square plan, depending on proportions, lies in the need for a larger plot of land and, as a result, more costly infrastructure.

The number of bedrooms that can be placed on a floor will guide interior design considerations in a rectangular design. Two categories can therefore be introduced: arrangements of either one bedroom or two side-by-side bedrooms. The width of a floor for a single bedroom occupying the dwelling's entire width can range from 12 feet (3.7 meters) to 14 feet (4.3 meters). The footprint of a floor needed to accommodate two adjacent bedrooms will range from 18 feet (5.5 meters) to 20 feet (6.1 meters) and larger.

The length of a dwelling will depend on several factors as well. In a typical subdivision, the common length of a lot is 100 feet (30 meters). When front and rear setbacks are considered, they will determine the length of a dwelling. The length of a structure will be at the designer's discretion and will depend on the functions that the unit will contain. When a narrow unit is designed, placing one or two rooms at one end of a bedroom floor, and one or two at the other end, will be a viable design option. The middle section can accommodate the service area of the floor such as stairs and bathroom. In the lower floor, placement of kitchen, dining area, and living room will be the determining criteria for the unit length. In a narrow home, when the length that these functions comfortably occupy is calculated, it can be as short as 32 feet (9.8 meters) to 40 feet (12 meters). The length of a dwelling can also be affected by the decision as to where to park a car. Indoor parking may require a longer footprint, whereas the length can be shorter when the parking arrangement is outdoors.

The question is, what might be a preferable width for a dwelling? A rectangular floor plate of 16 by 40 feet (4.8 by 12 meters) provides a great amount of modular options, allowing the installation of interior non-load-bearing or lightweight demountable partitions. With a narrow width, if prefabricated, transportation is simplified, and constructions costs kept low. Another great advantage of the dimensions is the opportunity to subdivide the 16 by 40 feet (4.8 by 12 meters) module into 16 by 20 feet (4.8 by 6 meters) 'half-modules' and create accessory rooms like garages, guest rooms, and/or rooftop solariums. On a larger scale, the width of allows builders to place it in a community as a detached or semi-detached structure or in a row of similar homes.

One of the distinguishing features of such design is the option extended to buyers of purchasing the type and 'quantity' of house that they need and can afford. This option is made possible by designing a three-story structure that can be built, sold, and inhabited as a single-family house, a duplex, or a triplex, thereby contributing to a healthy mix of user types in the same development. For example, in the case of a single-family 'model' house for a couple with one child, the ground floor can accommodate a living room, dining, washroom, laundry room, and kitchen, with plenty of storage, leaving the second level for three bedrooms, and a complete washroom with a bathtub. The semi-basement can be used as a garage and/or workshop. Countless configurations can be made with the same module, just changing the interior partitions, which can be installed by the manufacturer during production or the occupant after occupancy, considering the needs of the same family 20 years later, or another household completely, perhaps a single person: they can choose to rent their semi-basement as an independent unit with kitchen, living/dining area, bedroom, and washroom. On their two-level unit they may decide to expand the main bedroom and use the child's room as a home office, all with only minor difficulty or investment.

Adaptable housing was the aim of US firm Interface Studio Architects (ISA), who designed **Powerhouse**, a residential project that brings high-density housing to Francisville, Philadelphia, USA, using a mix of typologies that create a diverse community.

The varying heights of the buildings and the façades of brick, wood, and steel help integrate Powerhouse into the existing urban fabric. It allows infill to scale up to the proportions of the entire block while maintaining the character of the surrounding neighborhood. Unlike a typical infill development that contains a uniform housing model, Powerhouse includes a variety of dwelling types—single-family town houses, duplexes, bi-level live/work apartments, and one-story apartments—to attract homeowners and renters alike. The spatial organization of these create different levels of privacy while offering opportunities for social interaction between neighbors. Two apartment buildings, separated by a block of existing town houses, occupy one side of the street corner; the other contains alternating duplexes and town houses, with a staggered setback that avoids monotony in the street rhythm.

FUTURE HOMES FEATURES:

POWERHOUSE

→ High density
→ Adaptable to a range of occupants
→ Energy efficiency
→ Renewable energy sources

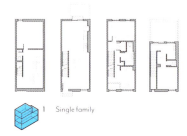

1 Single family

2 Duplex bi-level high

3 Duplex bi-level

5 Apartment bi-level live/work

5 Apartment bi-level

6 Apartment flat low

ISA designed the 'super stoop' for Powerhouse; it's a social space that expands the traditional town-house stoop and creates more opportunity for meetings between neighbors. A few sitting steps lead to the entrance of the lower duplex, while a couple more steps lead to the higher unit. Benches on the other side of the sidewalk offer temporary resting space facing the homes. The level changes create a dynamic meeting place in a small area.

Powerhouse was designed to comply with LEED Platinum certification. Green roofs form terraces that replace the traditional backyard, offering expansive views of the city while also managing stormwater. Rain gardens were designed along the curb lines for this purpose as well. Photovoltaic cells topping the roofs of the apartment buildings contribute toward the energy supply of the project. Triple-glazed windows, along with well-insulated walls, prevent heat from escaping the homes, reducing energy usage.

The design of Powerhouse introduces sustainable living to its inhabitants and the community and creates social spaces despite the density. The development draws young professionals, couples, and families to the growing neighborhood, demonstrating the makeup of a modern neighborhood that engages people of all backgrounds.

Adaptable designs are also the focus of **Woodview Mews**, a project in London, UK, built in 2015 and the first application of architecture firm Geraghty Taylor's LivinHome housing model. The design focuses on providing flexibility through layout and façade choices that can reflect its owners' lifestyles.

The LivinHome concept consists of three standard plans on open floor plates. One is an open-plan living space, another contains only bedrooms, and the third encompasses one- or two-bedroom apartments. The service zone of each layout is placed at the same location, which facilitates a change in plan when needed. At Woodview Mews, the six town houses are organized into 11 units of various densities—town houses, duplexes, and apartment. The ground floor features a recessed entryway, while the first and second floors have balconies.

A couple purchasing a town house may live in a duplex and rent out an apartment or live in an apartment and rent out two floors. When they decide to start a family, the town house can be reorganized to become their home. After the children grow up, the parents may rent out apartment floors to their children. They may also transform the ground floor into an office or shop. As they age, they may choose to enclose the balcony space to make room for an elevator. Using this method, aging in place is possible with minimal disturbance to the buildings and to neighbors.

Woodview Mews practices sustainability firstly by offering flexibility in accommodations, which encourages homeowners to stay with their current home and increases the lifespan of the development, which also saves money for the owners by avoiding the costs of moving to a larger home. The design standardization element of the LivinHome system can benefit from production to scale, resulting in savings from off-site construction and a cleaner construction process.

FUTURE HOME FEATURES:

WOODVIEW MEWS

→ **Adaptable to a range of occupants**

→ **Suited to multigenerational use**

→ **Prefabricated elements**

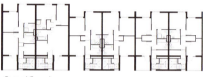
Second-floor plan

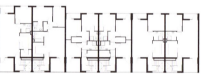
First-floor plan

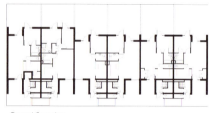
Ground-floor plan

Section

Flat   Duplex   House

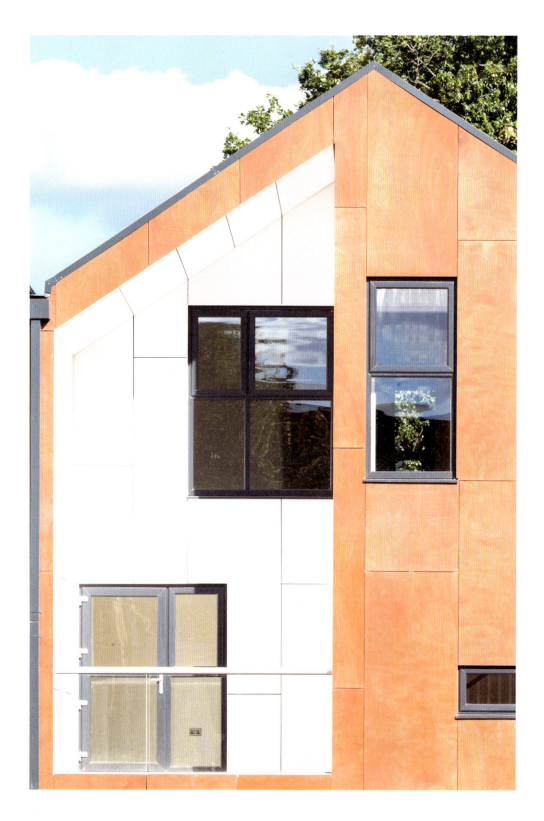

The ability to produce in larger volumes makes this system a good candidate for social housing; construction details could be recycled from site to site, further reducing waste, where it can prevent units standing vacant by transforming them into a type that is in demand.

An issue arose in discussions with the planning council during this project, due to the lack of policy accommodating buildings of hybrid use. Currently, the development can exist as its fixed 11 dwellings; if there is a change in layout, additional applications would be needed. While Woodview Mews pushes the boundaries of adaptability in the multifamily residential typology, it also highlights the issue of policy that is out of date with technology today.

FUTURE GARDENS

Conventional landscaping with turf, shrubs, and trees requires excessive amounts of water, maintenance, and chemicals, which results in resource depletion, energy consumption, pollution, and contamination. Due to a growing public and professional awareness, alternative practices such as edible landscaping and xeriscaping are taking hold in residences.

The most important aspect of maintaining an eco-friendly and sustainable garden is water efficiency. A properly designed outdoor space reduces water usage and chemical usage, requires little maintenance, and can be uniquely aesthetic. It can allow for a wide range of trees, shrubs, and flowering perennials to create an attractive and sensible yard.

Although the initial set-up for such a garden can seem expensive and daunting, the benefits reach far into the future. Personal benefits include money savings from chemicals and fertilizers as well as water use, in addition to saving time previously spent on maintaining the garden. These gardens also contain a unique aesthetic appearance, character, and message about the environment and our place in it.

XERISCAPED GARDENS

Variety of xeriscaped gardens

Examples of native plants used artistically.

Combination of drought-tolerant plants combined with a rain garden.

Creative use of downpipes leading to a large water tank for rainwater retention.

The aim of xeriscaping is water conservation through the creation of water-efficient landscapes. A properly designed outdoor xeriscape not only reduces water usage by 20 to 50 percent, but can also reduce chemical usage, requires little maintenance, and creates a unique aesthetic. Xeriscaping also allows for a wide range of trees, shrubs, and flowering perennials.

Before planting a xeriscape garden, it is important to lay out its overall organization. This involves negotiating the amount of land dedicated to turf, and creating water-use zones for plants that correspond to sun exposure and take advantage of the natural water flow. The overall goal is to reduce much of the land allocated to turf, while in turn increasing the efficiency of watering. A well-designed xeriscape should be self-sufficient after its first year of growth, which results in greatly reduced maintenance requirements in the long run.

Did You Know?

Simply put, xeriscaping is defined as the practice of landscaping to reduce, or eliminate, the need for irrigation.

WHICH PLANTS?

The selection of plant material is highly important in xeriscaping. Overall, it is necessary to select species that require little irrigation and maintenance. This means focusing on planting chiefly native species that have deeper root systems and can survive primarily on rainwater. These species should then be located in watering zones that were defined early on.

Native shrubs and trees are best since they are well adapted to the local rainfall levels, are pest-resistant, and are able to support themselves in drought through more complex root systems. Since climate conditions vary, it is important to contact local growing agencies to find out which perennials and plants will be best for xeriscaping.

Where turf is required it is important to avoid using conventional bluegrasses, which require a lot of water, and instead choose other hardier and water-efficient species like rye and fescue. Many of these species are almost identical to bluegrass but they tend to be softer underfoot and require little to no mowing or chemicals. Certain species of fescue, for instance, tend to have deeper roots than bluegrass and therefore retain their color even during droughts. They are frequently used in golf courses, sports fields, and parks, due to their deep green color and natural weed resistance.

PLANNING THE GARDEN

The organization of a xeriscape should also take into consideration the creation of water-use zones, or hydrozoning, to add efficiency to watering and reduce waste. Plants should be clustered together into zones that require frequent watering, occasional watering, or no watering at all to avoid over- or under-watering certain species. These zones should then be correlated with the sun. Zones that require lots of watering should be kept out of high-sun areas to reduce the amount of evaporation from the soil. Similarly, plants with low water requirements should be placed in areas with more sunlight. High-water-use zones should be limited in size and, if possible, be placed in highly visible areas such as entranceways due to the fact that these plants tend to be more aesthetically pleasing and lush.

The last concept involved in the organization of a garden is the topography and subsequent drainage patterns. Slopes that cause excessive runoff should be terraced to allow rainfall to seep into the ground for plant use, while low spots that drain poorly should either be avoided or amended to aid in their drainage. It is also possible to plant high-water-use plants in low spots, provided it is not too wet for the vegetation. By regarding the drainage patterns in the yard, the area may be customized with backfill and water redirected to where it is most needed.

Soil preparation is another important aspect of successful xeriscape design. Initially, it is important to assess the grade of soil currently in place by performing a drainage test. This involves digging a test planting hole and filling it with water. If it drains quickly, it needs to be filled up again. If this water remains within the hole for more than six hours, than the soil grade is low and should be improved for a xeriscape to function successfully. Soil grade can be improved first by amending it with organic and inorganic matter such as compost, peat, and sand to achieve a soil that has high water retention, but still drains excess water. Both compost and peat are used due to their high mineral content and high water-holding capacity, while sand is required to improve drainage and increase oxygen levels within the soil. It is best to mix these three compounds in relatively equal amounts and add them to the earth to encourage deep root growth.

Once the vegetation is planted, it is important to maintain the soil richness by aeration. Aeration increases water retention by reducing runoff, increases the oxygen levels within the soil for better growth, and also promotes deeper root growth. For thicker, clay-like soils as well as turf lawns, it is important to aerate twice a year in the spring and the fall, while xeriscape portions of the lawn only require aeration once a year due to their naturally higher water-retention capacity.

Finally, it is important to install effective irrigation in xeriscapes to facilitate maintenance as well as maximize water-usage efficiency. The best way to reduce the usage of hose water in irrigation is to obtain water through natural sources, such as rainwater runoff and gray water. Harvesting runoff water from downspouts, outbuildings, and paved surfaces, and then channeling it into a retention pond or rain barrels can add up to 26,000 gallons (100,000 liters) of saved water each year in temperate climate zones. This water should then be dispersed directly to the roots using a drip hose rather than a sprinkler due to the fact that sprinklers lose over a third of their water output to evaporation in-air and off the leaves of vegetation. It is also possible to design the water delivery drip system so that it delivers different amounts of water to different water-usage zones for maximum efficiency and minimal upkeep.

FUTURE HOMES FEATURES:

ROSS STREET HOUSE

→ Xeriscaped garden
→ Local materials
→ Sustainable utilities
→ Efficient insulation
→ Natural light and heating

A FUTURE HOUSE AND GARDEN

The low-water-demand garden is a highlight of **Ross Street House** in Madison, USA, the first home to be accredited with a LEED Platinum rating in the state of Wisconsin. In collaboration with her mechanical engineer husband, architect Carol Richard of Ross Street Design had always wanted to implement what she had learned during her career. Her own home offered an opportunity to do so. The house successfully blends in with other homes in the Glenway neighborhood, which consists of a mixture of post–World War II Cape Cod cottages.

The 2,700-square-foot (251-square-meter), three-story Ross Street House has a simple design. The architect provided detailed specifications for the planting of xeriscaped gardens in both the front and rear yards. With meticulously detailed drawings for paving and the planting, the landscape was transformed into an edible and low-water-demand garden. Plants such as wild strawberry, western sunflower, and herbs are just a few examples. Native perennial plants, which require minimal maintenance, were chosen for the garden.

To complement the exterior of neighboring houses and their proportions, the exterior walls are cladded with 6-inch (15.2-centimeter) tongue-and-groove cedar siding. The exterior walls are sprayed with foam insulation and the careful sealing of the windows and doors minimizes air infiltration to less than one air change per hour. Also, to maintain healthy indoor air, the house has a heat recovery ventilation system and a three-stage high-efficiency furnace.

During the design process, the architect aimed to meet LEED standards. To achieve this goal, an information model was created, and computer-aided design software was used. It helped to study the amount of daylight that could penetrate the house during the various seasons. With the main southern façade entirely opened, an ample amount of daylight is allowed to enter the house, while fixed louvers, strategically distanced, are designed to offer summer shade.

The open floor plan is finished with locally harvested materials such as maple wood flooring. The interior also has minimal details, light-colored walls and Energy Star appliances and fixtures. Furthermore, low-flow faucets and showerheads and dual-flush toilets are installed to reduce water consumption.

The three stories are connected by a central staircase that also lets natural light flow down. The private study and the bedroom are located on the top level, while the below-grade basement accommodates guests, mechanical fixtures, storage, and a Belgian-style beer brewing room. The living, kitchen, and dining spaces are organized on the main level in between.

While the Ross Street House integrates highly innovative green technologies without intruding on the aesthetics of the surrounding neighborhood, the house accommodates liveability for the occupants. It is worth noting that the house was honoured by the Madison Trust for Historic Preservation as the 2010 Future Landmark Award for Innovative New Design.

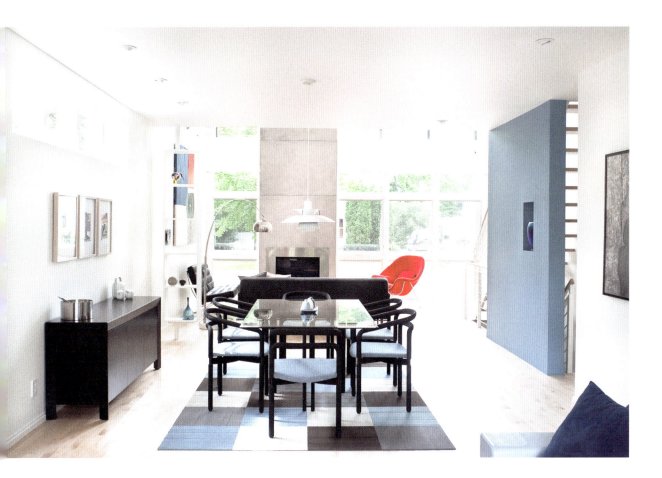

XERISCAPED GARDENS

INSIDE A FUTURE HOME:
SUSTAINABLE INTERIORS

When designing for the interior of a new home being built today, decisions need to be made about the internal layout, partitions, and storage methods, as well as the use of smart technology and energy-efficient systems and utilities.

As the demand for—and cost of—real estate rises in cities worldwide, and smaller dwellings become more common, one of the key challenges in designing new homes is to make spaces feel larger and comfortable. Storage is a related concern, and designers are continuing to come up with innovative ways of creating storage space within new homes.

The design and use of kitchens in particular has changed in recent decades, affected by changing lifestyle habits and technological innovations; the once humble room is now likely to be the center of the dwelling.

Energy efficiency is more important than ever as a result of climate change and rising energy costs, which will influence choices made about the kinds of heating, ventilating, and air-conditioning equipment installed in new homes. New ways of installing traditional utilities such as electricity and water are emerging, along with innovative and cost-effective ways to wire homes for telephone, cable TV, internet, and security systems.

When designing systems for new homes, home automation or 'smart technology' is increasingly part of the process. The growth of automation within the home has begun to shape the genesis of home designs and planning to be more inclusive of these technologies.

This section looks at all these considerations and offers examples of new homes that illustrate the possibilities available for home designers and builders.

ADAPTABLE INTERIORS

Interior design features that make small spaces seem larger, and contribute to their adaptability

Unobstructed circulation

Open plan

A rear deck as an outside room

Demountable partitions

Locating bathroom between spaces

Same size rooms

Taller spaces

Possible vertical connections

Efficient use of walls

Storage under stairs

Built-in furniture along the walls

Transparent materials

Non-defining floor covering

Natural light to spaces

As people around the world are increasingly living in cities, the need for living area—and its cost—is expected to rise. In response, designers and builders are concentrating more and more on designing dwellings that are relatively small yet comfortable. With a small dwelling, there are a variety of strategies that can be employed in interiors to make spaces feel larger and comfortable: typology, space distribution, flexibility, and choice of finishes are all important.

SPACES AND CIRCULATION

The functions in a home are commonly organized in zones—often designated as public, semi-public, and private. Public areas consist of the living and dining rooms, which can be used by the occupants and their guests. Semi-public areas are spaces such as the kitchens and bathrooms, while the bedrooms are considered private.

When space is at a premium, public rooms such as the rarely used formal dining room will not be included in a layout. An extended kitchen table, for example, can accommodate occupants and guests when needed. In the private zone, the placement of the bedrooms will depend on light, views, or noise and they will commonly be located on the upper floor of a house or the secluded part of an apartment. Regardless of whether the bedrooms are on upper or lower levels, the floor is naturally less open in plan and often has only a small hallway or limited circulation space.

The degree of connectivity between rooms will determine whether the spaces are public, semi-public, or private. A front entrance with a direct view of the living room will highlight the public nature of this space, whereas a closed corridor leading to a bedroom will reinforce privacy. So a passageway through a home needs to be designed as a comprehensive system that promotes efficiency, accessibility, and comfort. In small homes, interior horizontal and vertical circulation must be minimized so as not to take space away from living areas. Furthermore, front and rear access points, along with exterior paths, must be considered if appropriate connections are to be formed between interior and exterior spaces.

FLEXIBLE HOMES

Strategies to make a home more adaptable in the future begin with a suitable structural system. It is simpler to achieve greater flexibility when the structural support is limited to the two long walls of the house. Interior changes can then be made without concern for the structural integrity of the house.

In a small unit, rather than partitioning and creating spaces suitable for a single use it's ideal to keep the area free of interior partitions. Later, a partition may be built to separate space, add another bedroom, or add a home office. By keeping the floor initially open, the changes made as time passes will involve building rather than tearing down.

COLORS AND LIGHTS

Once the interior spaces of a home are created, finishing materials, furniture, and lighting can further contribute to its comfort and efficiency. The introduction of new products has led to new opportunities in interior design.

Color preferences vary according to individual taste, but certain colors tend to evoke spatial and emotional responses, regardless of individual preferences. Dark colors absorb light, and so they seem heavy in one's peripheral vision. When people look at dark walls, most feel that the wall must be closer to them than it is. The opposite is true of lighter walls. Similarly, rough textures such as unfinished wood or brick absorb more light and create shadows while light is reflected off smooth surfaces. As a result, smooth surfaces should be used in small spaces, and darker, textured surfaces should be avoided.

Lighting, both natural and artificial, can be a useful tool in dictating the size, atmosphere, and feel of a space. The quality of natural light within a home largely depends on a dwelling's orientation and the quantity and positioning of windows. An abundance of natural light within a home helps make small spaces feel larger and reduces the need for artificial lighting.

FUTURE HOME FEATURES:
CAMPBELL STREET

→ **Flexible interiors**
→ **Creative storage design**
→ **Natural lighting and ventilation**
→ **Maximized space**

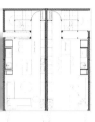

Third-floor plan   Rooftop plan

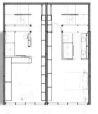 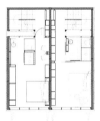

First-floor plan   Second-floor plan

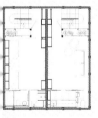 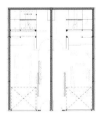

Basement plan   Ground-floor plan

Front elevation

Prefabricated, demountable walls can be used to enclose rooms with more permanent use. As a system of joined parts, the walls can be assembled, disassembled, and repositioned according to the need of the occupant. For example, two smaller bedrooms separated by a demountable wall will allow two children to each have their own room. When the older child moves out, the wall can be removed to make a larger space.

Maximizing space and allowing for flexible use was at the forefront when DKO Architecture and SLAB designed **Campbell Street**, an urban residential project in Melbourne, Australia, completed in 2017. Its neighborhood has a commercial and light industrial history; the street facing the houses consists of an eclectic mix of warehouses and town houses. The lot is 818 square feet (76 square meters) in size but fits two semi-detached dwellings, each with up to three bedrooms. To maximize space, the architects designed living areas for flexible use and incorporated natural lighting in interesting ways.

The two houses occupy six levels, each with a dedicated program. Living and entertainment areas of the house, which typically occupy the ground floor of a home, are instead placed on the topmost floors; this takes advantage of the building's height, offering more privacy and better views. A landscaped rooftop terrace and pool essentially resizes suburban living to a compact, urban scale. The master bedroom is on the second floor, with a generous distance from street-level activities. The levels below are more flexible in program. The first floor can function as a playroom if there are children in the household, or it can be converted to a bedroom through the hidden bed; the basement theater can be transformed in the same way. Smart storage is also integrated into these rooms for spatial efficiency. Creative details are included in the homes, such as a timber chopping block in the kitchen, which can be moved to allow for increased dining capacity, and a laundry chute connected from each bedroom level to the basement.

The designers wanted to have natural light penetrating each level of the homes, especially the basement; the architects achieved this by adding a light well in the staircase. On aboveground floors, a custom punctured metal screen on the street façade serves a double purpose. During the day, they can be opened fully to allow in sunlight, or partly to block direct sun. At night, they can be closed to give an extra layer of privacy, and the interior lighting peeking through the screen makes for a characteristic façade.

The architects of Campbell Street introduced methods for layout, lighting, and storage to create an optimal living space for homeowners of various lifestyles. As available housing area in urban districts slowly declines, Campbell Street exemplifies how to maximize usable space on small city lots.

FUTURE HOMES

ADAPTABLE INTERIORS

Another interesting project that shows a forward-thinking use of space and layout is **Whittaker Cube**, in Kakanui, New Zealand, designed in 2016 for clients who wished to maximize views toward the sea and privacy from the street and the neighboring houses. The architects at Dravitzki Brown adopted an unconventional floor plan and strategic placements to fulfill the client's needs, all in a compact cube with a footprint of 25 by 25 feet (8 by 8 meters).

The house consists of two levels, one dedicated to public functions and the other for private quarters. Rather than place the living area on the ground floor as in a typical house, in Whittaker Cube the floor functions are switched. Having bedrooms on the lower level provides more privacy for the homeowners, since most of the property has a fence around it that covers the ground floor from view. This also gives the living area greater views to the surroundings due to the height. Windows are mostly placed on the sides facing the sun, with sea views; this allows the house to benefit from an abundance of natural light and passive heat gains.

Whittaker Cube is roughly two-thirds the size of a typical New Zealand home. It can fit the same program on a more restrictive area due to its efficient use of space. On the first floor, normal doors are replaced with sliding ones to reduce space taken up by open doors, while the second floor is purely open plan. The home contains one large bathroom that serves the two-bedroom house, eliminating the footprint and need for utility connections taken up by another washroom. Circulation space is minimized to just the staircase, with the only hallway also functioning as the entry to the home. The laundry room is only accessible outdoors, but due to the master bedroom's separate direct entrance it is only steps away. These space-saving strategies result in two large, spacious bedrooms, and an adequately sized office. It also allowed the architects to use the saved costs toward a more detailed façade system and more durable materials. The house is clad in cedar, functioning as a rainscreen that gains more character with weather and age. The interiors incorporate American oak to echo the wooden façade.

The architects showcase ways of conserving area to create a light and spacious feeling, making the most out of the seaside plot and achieving a lot in a tiny footprint.

FUTURE HOME FEATURES:

WHITTAKER CUBE

➔ **Innovative façade**
➔ **Flexible interiors**
➔ **Natural lighting and ventilation**
➔ **Maximized space**

First-floor plan

Ground-floor plan

SMART STORAGE

One of the challenges faced by occupants in contemporary homes can be summed up with one word: stuff. As a result of rampant consumerism, the need for storage space has grown in recent years and it is expected to do so even more in the future. When a space, regardless of its size, is clean and uncluttered, it will seem larger. As a result, innovative storage solutions are increasingly becoming available.

An obvious solution to lack of storage space is to get rid of unused items or not to have them in the first place, a responsibility that falls on the homeowners. But for the designer considering storage requirement in their design, the task is to find a fit between the occupants and their storage needs. A traditional approach to the design of storage in homes is to consider it part of the room's space. For example, a closet will be an integrated part of a bedroom area. In other spaces, it's possible to place purchased freestanding storage cabinets or have them fabricated custom-made for a specific spot.

While a small home may not have the same storage capacity as a big one, treating space as a valuable commodity is a key strategy to an efficient and organized design. Strategically located shelving and closets will optimize the storage potential of a unit without interfering with living spaces.

Recent demographic transformation and new lifestyle trends have seen changes in living habits and, as a result, storage needs. A single person's household does not need as much storage as a household with children; nor, at times, can they afford it. Some owners may want to have an open storage with no front doors in some spaces while others may want to keep these same items guarded and locked. In kitchen design, for example, some like the cabinets to have solid doors, while others may want them to be glassed and a few might not want to have doors at all. Designing for choice will therefore be a key to future storage design.

NEW STORAGE IDEAS

Built-in storage units can be costly, yet those that suit the specific needs of the occupant are often worth the investment. New directions in storage design and fabrication see a fit between occupants and their storage needs at a conception phase. A catalog of different storage modules can provide a range of sizes and designs that can accommodate, among other things, TV, library, pantry, and a home office. In addition, the garage, one of the home's overlooked areas, can integrate storage modules and a work bench where repair and maintenance work can be carried out, transforming that area into a multipurpose space in addition to parking a car.

Choosing from a catalog of storage options will be no different than choosing the dwelling size and layout. In the process of buying the home, the buyer will choose the number of storage items, their configuration, and preferred location. In prefabricated modular production, the storage elements will be assembled in the plant and transported to the site with the chosen storage elements ready for occupancy. Such processes guarantee that a homebuying household will select and pay only for storage components that they need and can afford and can select the preferred material and color. To maximize storage potential, shelves, drawers, baskets, and rods can be used to allow the occupant to accommodate an entire wardrobe, often eliminating the need for additional armoire or chest of drawers, thereby saving space and money.

Innovations in computer programing and digital manufacturing allows all this to happen. The buyer may sit with a sales representative and choose their needed storage elements and find their cost while adjusting their choices according to their budget. Storage fabricators can optimize their production by translating requests from a sales center into the factory floor for a timely delivery.

The development of digital technologies such as 3D printing, along with demographic changes, will likely force additional innovations that will see our storage methods at home change.

Space Dividers

Furniture partitions are increasingly being used as space dividers that work in several ways to increase efficiency and comfort. Using storage or shelving systems to divide spaces reduces the need for interior partition walls. Additionally, furniture partitions help to make small spaces feel larger by blurring boundaries between rooms, allowing the eye to see beyond them, preventing a boxed-in feeling.

Designing creative storage was an integral part of the process for **3500 Millimetre House** in South Jakarta, Indonesia, designed for the architect's family by AGo Architects in 2018. As the name suggests, the house has a width of only 11.5 feet (3.5 meters), and with only three stories to fit all family home functions finding space for storage was an issue. Through discussions negotiating what the family needed, and clever storage solutions, the architects were able to design a comfortable-sized home for a family of three.

The master bedroom is on the ground floor, allowing social spaces, the son's bedroom and his play space to benefit from higher views. Although the house has distinct floors, there are additional levels between them that blur the divisions, creating one cohesive space throughout. The staggered levels allow for a double-height living area, creating a more spacious atmosphere. The façade of the home is a screen of perforated steel and polycarbonate, filtering the sunlight that reaches in. Behind the façade is a space that feels neither indoor or outdoor. Plants grown in this transition space connect it with the exterior while bringing nature into the home.

The architects chose sustainable and cost-efficient materials for the home, using wood for all interior fixtures. This furthers the coherence between the different spaces of the house. The architects strived to eliminate walls, choosing instead to integrate storage in dividers and stairs. The kitchen island contains cabinets

FUTURE HOME FEATURES:

3500 MILLIMETRE HOUSE

→ Creative storage solutions
→ High-density living
→ Affordable materials
→ Green spaces

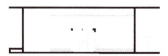
Third-floor plan

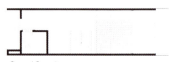
Second-floor plan

First-floor plan

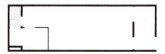
Ground-floor plan

SMART STORAGE

SMART STORAGE

on two sides, as well as a set of cupboards above it; the living area has built-in storage beneath the wooden 'floor' surrounding the sofa; the TV console and additional storage is nestled into the stairs going up from the living area; the son's bed is raised above a study space; and more storage shelves are tucked behind stairs. These storage solutions make each element of the house multifunctional, reducing clutter.

The plug-in storage system described above can transform the narrow home into a more spacious experience, combined with the level changes and abundance of natural light. The 3500 Millimetre House is an example of urban living that is dense, yet comfortable.

Innovative storage is also at the heart of **Mills House**. Designed for a mother and her newborn son, it is an extension to a one-story house in Melbourne, Australia, that was designed in anticipation of the family's needs. In 2016 Austin Maynard Architects transformed the ground floor of the home into a giant toy box, creating a fun environment for the baby to grow up in. The original façade and two of the rooms were kept, separated from the extension by a central light well.

The existing rooms were converted into a bedroom, study, and bathroom, leaving the rest of the ground level for a combined living, dining, and kitchen area. The floor in this open-plan space is raised by 1.5 feet (45 centimeters), an ideal height for seating and ideal depth for storage. The architects eliminated cupboards, which take up horizontal space in an already narrow site. Instead, they are rotated to become toy boxes on the ground, causing minimum disturbance as it becomes the new flooring. The coverage area of this floor creates an abundance of storage that hides clutter in the home. The lounge area is sunken so that the edges of the boxes become seats, or a surface for children to play on. The kitchen and dining area sit above the platform. The kitchen island is raised another 1.5 feet, on one side bordered by the ground and on the other by the raised floor and equally high courtyard. This allows the mother to cook from one side of the counter and for her son to help her from the other, and also provides easy access to ingredients from the courtyard garden.

In addition to spatial connections on the ground floor, the architects designed for interactions between the floors. A perforated steel staircase, connected to the upper-floor corridor of the same material, establishes visual and acoustic connections; in this way, mother and son can communicate easily. The lightweight material also gives a delicate feel, increasing the spaciousness of the home.

The architects designed with the family in mind, especially considering how the baby would grow up in this environment. With the extension, it becomes a fun childhood home where mother and son can create great memories. Mills House showcases how storage can change the spatial experience of a home.

FUTURE HOME FEATURES:

MILLS HOUSE

→ **Creative storage solutions**
→ **High-density living**
→ **Flexible use of interior space**
→ **Visual and acoustic connections**

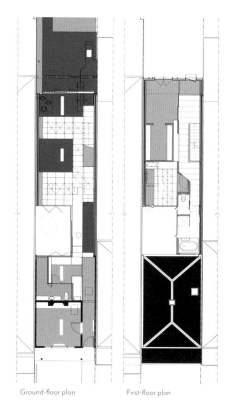

Ground-floor plan   First-floor plan

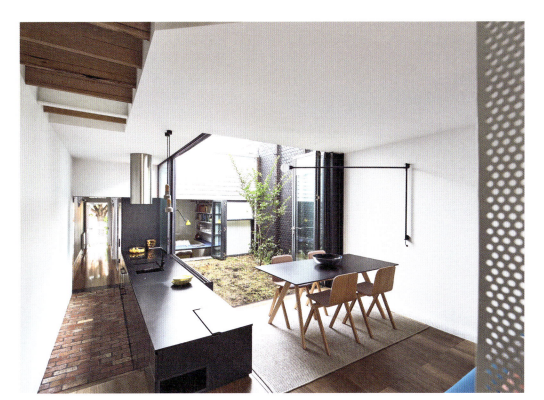

SMART STORAGE

FUTURE HOMES

SMART STORAGE

FUTURE KITCHENS

Features that improve the sustainability of the kitchen

1. Recycling waste
2. Growing food
3. Compostability
4. Recycled material
5. Energy star appliances
6. Natural light
7. Family space
8. Energy-efficient windows

FUTURE HOME FEATURES:

SURRY HILLS HOUSE

→ Kitchen as social hub
→ Open-plan design
→ Natural lighting

Ground-floor plan

First-floor plan

The design and use of kitchens have changed remarkably in recent decades. Changes can be attributed primarily to the transformation of lifestyle habits and new technological innovations. It is reasonable to assume that these changes are likely to continue as the dwelling on its subcomponents is becoming more sustainable and new environmentally sensitive materials and advanced construction methods are incorporated.

PROGRESSIVE TRANSFORMATION

The arrival of the baby boom cohort to the housing market in the 1980s saw the demand for homes further exceed supply. Boomers were eager to spend on comforts, and kitchen appliances were part of this trend. Homeowners turned the kitchen into one of the house's showpieces. In North America for example, an island was added with a broiling top for indoor barbecues and a second service sink was introduced, as were a bar-like seating arrangement and a breakfast area.

With dining rooms becoming less used, the kitchen has turned into the home's social space. The open-plan concept has taken on a new meaning, turning the entire floor, or most of it, into one large area, with several functions feeding into the kitchen. Homework, home accounting, reading, watching TV, and entertaining friends all take place in this space. Kitchens have also annexed adjacent rooms; kitchen–family room, kitchen–media room, and kitchen–home office are some of the popular layouts.

Turning the kitchen into the family's social center necessitated further upgrades in appearance. Manufacturers paid more attention to form and design, calling in top industrial designers to turn bulky appliances into design masterpieces. Clad in stainless-steel facings, black edges, and digital readouts, appliances took on a slick look.

The Sub-Zero company moved the fridge motor to the top, which helped reduce its depth and make it look like part of the cabinets. A programmable oven-fridge was designed catered to the needs of households on the move, keeping dinners cool until it was time to start cooking, and the food warm until the family arrived before dinnertime.

A dual dishwasher has eliminated the need to place the dishes back in the cabinet—one compartment washes while the other stores—and in a dual-compartment oven two items can be cooked at different temperatures simultaneously.

An example of the kitchen as a multi-use social space can be seen in **Surry Hills House**, a renovation and addition project in Sydney, Australia, designed by Benn & Penna Architecture in 2015. The town house previously sat small and cramped on its narrow and long site. The architects redesigned the spatial organization of the house while expanding it with the aim of fully integrating indoor and outdoor living. Only the outer walls of the original structure were kept and internal partitions were moved and removed to add new bedrooms, bathrooms, kitchen, courtyard, and living spaces.

The home is divided into its public and private spaces spread over two floors, with features optimized for its programs. The upstairs bedrooms and bathrooms are split by a series of horizontal divisions, creating spaces with privacy and views. The ground floor is free of partitions, facilitating a continuous spatial flow between the living area, kitchen, and dining area. The staircase is designed to be the center of the plan, with a skylight above to bring sunlight down to the ground floor. The open plan and natural lighting create a more enjoyable space for socializing and relaxing.

The kitchen is in the rear, leading out to the courtyard. The architects erased the boundary between these two spaces by continuing the kitchen counter out for the entire length of the yard that effectively extends the kitchen into the outdoors. Fully transparent folding patio doors serve as the back wall, minimizing the divide when closed and completely erasing it when opened. The extension of this space is made possible with a retractable panel that connects to the glass doors to create a complete seal. Essentially, this integrates the cooking and eating functions of the home with outdoor living, producing a central hub for social activity. Surry Hills House explores the full potential of the narrow site; with the open-plan ground floor, the architects were able to showcase how spatial organization can be used to create effective and inviting social spaces.

Tenhachi House in Kanagawa, Japan, is another example of a modern kitchen space that is incorporated into other parts of the house. The project was a renovation of an apartment, designed by husband-and-wife architects at Tenhachi Architect & Interior Design for their family and completed in 2015. The apartment was originally divided into several rooms, but for the renovation the architects stripped down all interior walls and ceiling, revealing the concrete structure to facilitate a more spacious, open-plan home. Private areas (apart from the toilet) are defined not by walls, but rather by open boxes. These cubes act as connectors between private areas and the more public living area. The bedroom box divides the space vertically in two. Below is the main bed space, while above is a lofted child's space, accessed by a ladder. The bathroom box is left open on one side, the only divider being a white curtain. This provides enough privacy while maintaining the spacious feeling of an open plan.

A 14.8-foot (4.5-meter) table made of Japanese cedar acts as the centerpiece of the living space. The table runs through the kitchen, dining, and workspace areas for both adults and children. There are no physical divisions between each program, allowing for the space to be used flexibly. The functional layout of the table may change throughout the day, from breakfast, to after school, to a dinner gathering. A sink and stovetop occupy one half of the table. The kitchen is completed with storage in floor-to-ceiling cabinetry on the nearby wall as well as overhanging shelves above the table. The opposite side of the space is for working, where a computer can be placed. Storage is also available below, supported by a row of bookshelves, easily accessible for children. The table becomes the dining area during mealtime, and can accommodate seating for 20 people. Tenhachi Architects personalized their apartment in this thorough renovation, which brings all members of the family together.

FUTURE HOME FEATURES:
TENHACHI HOUSE

→ **Furniture partitions**
→ **Open-plan design**
→ **Creative storage**
→ **Flexible spaces**

Floor plan

ENERGY EFFICIENCY

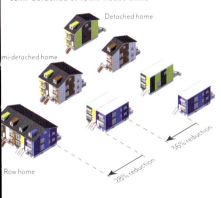

Substantial reduction in energy consumption will be made when dwelling units are built as semi-detached or town-house units

Measures that increase home energy efficacy

1   Insulation to avoid condensation
2   Double glazing with low-E coating
3   Windows with thermal break
4   External insulation to avoid thermal bridges
5   Underfloor insulation
6   Area of operable windows equivalent to 5% of floor area

Global environmental challenges such as climate change, as well as rapidly rising energy costs, are fueling a drive toward more energy-efficient dwellings. As a result, designers and home owners are paying more attention to the kinds of advanced heating, ventilating, and air-conditioning equipment they install. But which systems are really the most energy efficient?

Today, houses are much more energy efficient due to advanced building science, and innovative products and techniques. Moreover, because building envelopes are more airtight, concern for air quality has increased as well.

Central systems commonly require limited space and must be attached to a network of conduits to force the air through the house. Convection systems, such as ductless heat pumps, electric baseboard heaters, and fan-assisted room heaters, are more flexible and are located inside the house. The ductless heat pump, on the other hand, is usually installed on exterior walls close to the ceiling.

A factor to consider when selecting a heating or cooling system is the available energy. Naturally, energy from renewable sources would be much preferred. In addition, one must be aware of the local cost of natural gas and electricity before deciding to install any system, as the energy rates can greatly affect the life-cycle cost of the system.

TYPES OF SYSTEMS

In general, heating and cooling systems can be divided into three categories based on their source of energy. The sources can be fossil fuels, renewable, and biomass. Electrical systems use electricity as their source of power. Since all the energy put into the system is transformed to heat, except energy used by fans and other such devices, their gross efficiency is commonly rated at 100 percent. In the electrical system, a current is passed through a resistor that, in turn, generates heat.

The permanently mounted electric baseboard heater is probably the most common type of room heater. Ideally installed under windows, they have a 100 percent gross efficiency. However, their effectiveness is significantly compromised, since only a portion of the heat delivered is used to heat the air.

A heat pump is designed to transfer energy from one place to another; geothermal and air-source pumps are the main types. These systems are increasingly popular due to the high level of comfort they bring and because of their high efficiency. Another appealing characteristic is their reversibility; a heat pump cools or heats the home depending on the season.

The geothermal heat pump, also called a ground-source heat pump, is a device that uses ground water as a heat source or a heat sink. Looped pipes containing a liquid are installed in the ground and the system transfers the energy available from the ground to the interior of the home or vice versa. A central heating unit, usually located in the basement of the house, forces conditioned air through the duct network into the home.

HERE COMES THE SUN

Considering and incorporating the effects of the sun on buildings into a design may reduce energy consumption by as much as 30 percent. Maximizing natural light and energy gains is important year-round, while orienting the house for passive solar gain can assist during winter. Houses should be sited in an east–west direction, such that one of the main façades faces south (north in the southern hemisphere). However, since in the northern hemisphere winter heating is a bigger concern than summer cooling, orientations as close as possible to due south are recommended, ideally within 10 degrees west of south (10 degrees west of north in the southern hemisphere). This slight westerly direction is most beneficial as the sun's intensity peaks early in the afternoon and not when the sun reaches its midday zenith.

Diagrammatic representation of district heating

The air-source heat pump draws heat from the outside air during the heating season and dumps heat outside during the cooling season. There are two possibilities with this category of systems: the central unit and the ductless unit. The central unit is composed of an outside heat exchanger attached to an indoor central unit that forces air through a duct network. The ductless heat pump system is composed of an outside heat exchanger and several wall-mounted units inside the house, and therefore no duct network is required. The units are connected through pipes running inside the walls and should ideally be installed on exposed walls.

Ceiling-mounted fan-assisted units are also popular. In addition to circulating the air for better effectiveness and comfort, some systems include a pre-heat device to reduce energy consumption. The heating element is consistently kept at a 'ready to heat' temperature to reduce the electrical load generated when initiating the heating of a resisting element.

Airflow in the Home

A ventilation system is a device that replaces stale and humid air by allowing fresh air inside the building. Codes in many jurisdictions stipulate that every newly constructed home must be equipped with a mechanical ventilation system to provide air changes in different parts of the house. For example, a small home may require a total airflow of 10 gallons per second (40 liters per second) combined with one third of an air change every hour. A substantial amount of heat can be lost in the process. Designs that use traditional building methods such as cross ventilation are based on the Chimney Effect whereby the air enters at the bottom and exits on top, as well as Heat Recovery Ventilators (HRV), which transfer heat from existing to incoming air. These are preferable since they are more sustainable.

GETTING OFF THE GRID

Gaining all energy from off-the-power-grid sources was the aim of **Hunter's Point**, a net-zero housing development by Pearl Homes in Cortez, southwest Florida, USA, on the Gulf of Mexico. The design was led by architect Beth McDougal in collaboration with the Florida Solar Energy Center, a research institute at the University of Central Florida. It is one of the first communities in the USA to combine net-zero capabilities with home automation. The goal was to build a single-family residence with positive carbon footprint that could run entirely on solar power and would generate more energy than the owner can consume.

FUTURE HOME FEATURES:
HUNTER'S POINT

→ Smart technology
→ Energy efficiency
→ Automated systems
→ Maximized space

The developers focused on building responsibly, using sustainable materials and providing an off-grid power supply solution. Utilizing the most common and free natural resource in Florida—solar power, the Sonnen home battery systems create an independent source. In case of a storm, the local power grid is likely to fail, and a vast majority of homeowners will face temporary outages of a few hours, days, or even weeks. The homes at Hunter's Point are equipped with an 'intelligent system' providing clean, carbon-neutral energy. They also feature the Broan Nutone's Overture System Smart Air Quality Monitor Room Sensors, a fully automated fresh-air system. This device uses smart sensors that automatically detect temperature, humidity, volatile organic compounds, and CO_2 to help control indoor air quality by activating the home's ventilation devices to replace stale and polluted air with fresh, clean air.

Hunter's Point promises to be the first LEED Zero-certified, sustainable community in Florida. The development includes 86 net-zero, solar-powered houses and 47 boat slips on the near 18-acre (7.3-hectare) property. The planning also follows the Green Building Council's LEED native landscaping requirements. Every home has centrally located Guardian IQ2 Panel. From lighting control to heating and air conditioning, to smart irrigation and home security, this feature creates a smart home with serious green credentials.

The homes' interior measures 1,650 square feet (165 square meters). The ground floor consists of a two-car garage and storage space. The second floor includes kitchen, dining and living areas, a powder room, and a private patio, and the third floor has three bedrooms.

Hunter's Point demonstrates the possibility of living a comfortable lifestyle that at the same time drastically reduces carbon footprint. The developer, Pearl Homes, has plans to build similar communities and create a real impact on decarbonizing the world.

FUTURE HOMES

ENERGY EFFICIENCY

FUTURE HOME FEATURES:
LIMESTONE HOUSE

→ **Energy efficiency**
→ **Local materials**
→ **Prefabricated components**
→ **Passivhaus standard**

Individual homes, as well as developments, are being designed for energy efficiency. **Limestone House**, designed by John Wardle Architects, is a sustainability focused single-family home in Melbourne, Australia. Completed in 2018, the house was built to Passivhaus and Living Building Challenge (LBC) standards through a careful selection of materials and design decisions to ensure low energy usage and low carbon impact.

The two-story house is private toward the street, but has large openings on the opposite, northern face to take advantage of optimal sun angles. The living areas on the first floor are arranged around a courtyard and planted pond that forms the center of the home. A study floats above the pond, providing a moment of serenity. Upstairs contains the private quarters of the house.

As material selection was a crucial aspect of the LBC, John Wardle Architects chose to use largely local resources, with a focus on recycled materials. Mount Gambier limestone, a stone that ages with character, was used for façades of the home. Repurposed blackbutt timber from a neighboring state was chosen to complement the limestone, as it turns silver gray with age. Internal timber was sourced from reclaimed eucalyptus. Using local and repurposed materials ensured low embodied energy and reduced carbon emissions through transportation.

Limestone House achieved a Passivhaus certification by using airtight construction and high-performing insulation, with triple glazing used for windows. As a result, the home requires very little energy usage toward heating or cooling, maintaining a comfortable indoor temperature year-round. Airtight construction was realized through prefabrication, which reduced construction waste and provided a clean environment for taped seals to ensure quality. As components were being manufactured off-site, the basement was being built to cut down construction time. In achieving the LBC, the house has self-management of water and wastewater; it is also self-sufficient in energy production, with a photovoltaic cell system that produces more energy than the house uses. The results of the two building standards work together—the Passivhaus standard for insulation reduces reliance on energy for heating, which in turn facilitates meeting the LBC standard for energy generation.

Limestone House provides a great example of formal and material explorations in designing within the constraints of green construction standards.

First-floor plan

Ground-floor plan

Basement plan

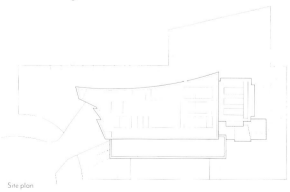

Site plan

ENERGY EFFICIENCY

FUTURE HOMES

SUSTAINABLE UTILITIES

'Utilities' is an all-encompassing term that refers to the home's subsystems that link a dwelling to the city's infrastructure and service the occupants to reflect the many necessities of modern life. In addition to electricity, fresh water supply, and drainage, homes are now being fed by and wired for telephone, cable TV, internet, and security systems, among others. To increase efficiency, and save cost and time, innovative ways to install utility conduits in new and existing dwellings are worth considering.

PLUMBING

Once the dwelling's rough structure has been constructed, installation of the home's plumbing system begins. Three main components make up the system: water supply, water and waste removal, and fixtures through which the water is used. Currently the installation of plumbing is determined by the location of what is known as the 'wet functions' that include bathrooms, kitchens, and laundry room. The process in wood-frame construction can be costly since prior to the installation, the plumber needs to perform preparatory work that includes drilling in floor joists and wall studs.

Several innovations were introduced over the past few decades in plumbing installation, yet their full implementation is often difficult as the industry in many nations is governed by often hard-to-change codes which take a long time to alter. When attempting to find an alternative to current practice, one needs to bear in mind that any change will have to be approved by local code officials. Yet new products are constantly being introduced including PEX plastic pipes that replace the traditional steel and copper ones and simplify connection between components.

Innovation in the installation of subsystems in future homes is likely to address the efficiency issue and shorten the time it takes to install. The first step will see rational location of the wet functions. When possible, it will make more sense to cluster them together, which will shorten the length of the conduits to reach them. When two functions are located back to back—say the kitchen and bathroom or two bathrooms—the wall between them can be specially designed and fabricated to contain pipes to permit easy access to those pipes in the future.

The next step will see the placement of all the main conduits to include pipes, electric wire, and air-conditioning ducts in the same location to facilitate easy installation as well as their replacement and maintenance. The use of open-web joists for the building of floors in wood-frame homes can help create a canal for these conduits on each floor to run along the long dimension of the structure. These pipes will link the house to the municipal water and sewer networks and to the electrical power entry. These main pipes split into smaller feeding pipes that lead mains water and remove wastewater in each bathroom and the kitchen, for example.

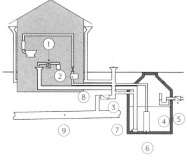

A diagram of a dwelling's water harvesting and recycling system

1. Solenoid valve
2. Pump control
3. Underground filter
4. Cistern
5. Anti-surcharge
6. Pressure pump
7. Inflow smoothing filter
8. Anti-surcharge
9. Public storm/sewer line

SAVING WATER

When purchasing home appliances, their water performance needs to be closely examined as some consume more water than others in their operation. Dishwashers and clothes washers need to be studied before purchase, not only for their energy efficiency but also for their water consumption. The initial cost of more energy-efficient washers might be slightly higher, but they will be cost savers in the long run.

A wall canal along the floor can accommodate electric wiring and simplify their maintenance

FUTURE HOME FEATURES:
CATSKILLS HOUSE

→ Energy-efficient systems
→ Natural light and heating
→ Affordable materials
→ Radiant tubes beneath the flooring

Floor plan

ELECTRICAL SYSTEMS

Another domestic system where installation methods are likely to be improved is electrical. The system is commonly made up of wires, switches, and plugs. At present the process of installing electricity in a wood-frame home is much like plumbing in that it involves the passage of wires in the middle point of the wall where the electrician needs to drill a hole in each stud that make a wall as well as the floor or ceiling joist, a time-consuming process.

When the system needs to be upgraded or maintained, adding or replacing a wire is almost impossible and often requires removing the wall's covering. A different approach can emulate technologies used in commercial applications such as office partitions. A specialized hollow molding can run in the wall along the spot where the wall meets the floor. The face of that molding will accommodate plugs and from there vertical conduits will reach the light switches.

INNOVATIONS IN UTILITIES

Innovations in utility installation and delivery are expected to transform the way we construct homes and serve them with utilities. Homes are already being built around the world that are dealing with utilities in new ways.

An energy-efficient geothermal heating system was designed to serve **Catskills House**, designed by husband-and-wife firm J_spy Architecture in 2017. The house is their relaxing family retreat in the Catskills Mountains in New York, USA, and although the site is expansive, the couple decided to only build on a small portion of it, cutting down energy costs. The home is industrial and unassuming on the outside, yet welcoming and comfortable on the inside.

The massing of the home comes from four essential blocks. Three concrete boxes combine to form the ground level of the home. Two of the blocks each contain the private and public functions, with the entrance tucked in between the two. A third, smaller, block serves as a mechanical room. Although the interiors of the living room are clad in concrete as a continuation of the exterior façade, the juxtaposition with large, floor-to-ceiling windows brings natural light and warmth into the home. A fourth metal box, which rests on top to heighten the main living area, provides spaciousness. Extending from this room is an expansive patio with unobstructed views of the surrounding landscape.

Due to the remote location of the house, the only utility available on site was electricity. The architects wished to use a more energy-efficient way to heat the home, in the end deciding on a geothermal heat pump, connected to a 400-foot (122-meter) well that provides heating. This is joined with a layer of hydronic radiant tubes beneath the flooring to ensure even warmth throughout the house. During the summer time, ducted-system air conditioning is employed. These two systems together drastically reduce the electricity bill for the family. The substantial overhang of the metal box also plays a part, reducing solar gain in the summer. The home is also equipped with high-performing insulation and a tankless hot-water system to further cut down energy usage.

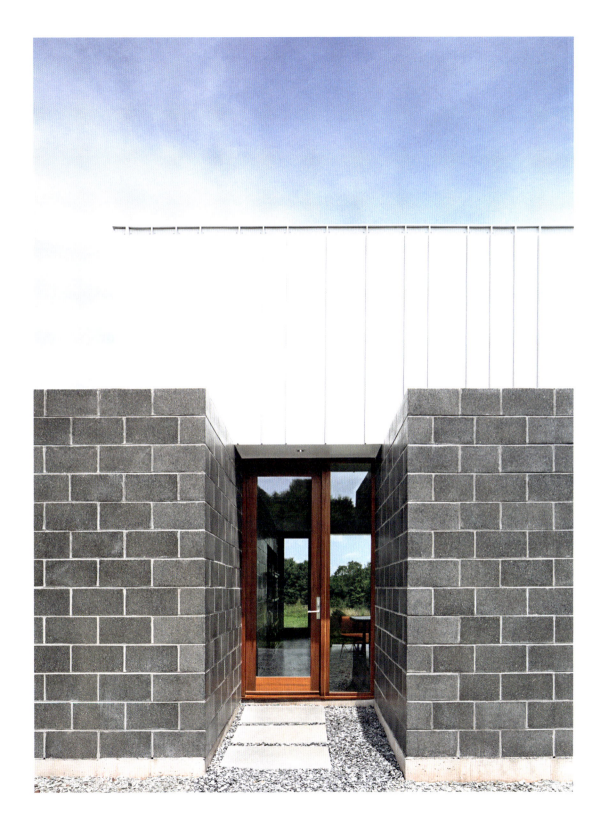

An innovative system of water delivery and circulation is one of the highlights of **Holmberg House**, built in 2016 in an urban district of Belgrano, Argentina, for a young couple and their two children. Architects Estudio Borrachia integrated nature into various spaces of the home to create a wholesome environment for the children to grow up in. The perimeter of the home is wrapped in a façade of pipes that circulate water for the family's use.

The social programs of the ground floor are organized around three outdoor spaces. The first is a front yard transitioning from the street to the house entrance. The back garden contains a pool for the family to enjoy. The third is a pond, bordering the kitchen and the dining space. Along with the living area, they are open plan, allowing maximum natural light to permeate the ground floor through the fully glazed walls. The same walls envelop the first and second floors, providing abundant cross ventilation for the private quarters of the home.

There are two storage tanks for water in the home. One is located on the ground floor, in a shaded space to maintain a cool temperature; the tank for hot water is situated on the roof, directly connected to solar panels that heat it, without reliance on the grid. In the winter, this tank acts as a heat barrier, preventing heat loss from the roof to cut down energy usage. The façade resembles a giant radiator, transmitting heat from the water it carries. It also provides support for plants grown on it and in the green spaces, creating microclimates for nature to thrive in. After a period of living in the home, the owners found various species of plants and animals on the site. The pipe façade also filters light entering the home, creating interesting effects on both sides of it. The design of the home can also maintain privacy through this as well.

Holmberg House's façade of piping is the central element of many home functions that revolve around it. Through this unique system, the architects were able to bring natural living to an urban context.

FUTURE HOME FEATURES:

HOLMBERG HOUSE

→ Solar heating
→ Green space
→ Natural light and ventilation
→ Energy-efficient systems

Terrace

Second-floor plan

First-floor plan

Ground-floor plan

SUSTAINABLE UTILITIES

SUSTAINABLE UTILITIES

SMART TECHNOLOGY

Digital features of networked cities

nnected buildings

Emergency

Public access

ıtelligent vehicle

Health and wellbeing

Social media

As technology continues to advance at an ever-accelerating pace, the prevalence of home automation will only increase. In a few short years, the sheer variety of home automation technology available to the everyday consumer has expanded, and the functionality of automation technology has improved to ease the daily lives of users. The growth of automation within the home has begun to influence home designs and planning to be more inclusive of these technologies.

When automation technology first entered the consumer market, security was one of the key topics. Suddenly, the average consumer was able to network their entire home with their own security system. While rudimentary at first, this technology grew to include elements like motion sensors, high-pitched alarms, and eventually cameras. Home security cameras allowed users to be able to remotely monitor activity in their house to safeguard against intruders, accidents, and theft. The popularity of such technology began a trend of innovation toward creating a ubiquitous home environment.

'Smart technology,' a moniker usually assigned to technology aimed at making daily life easier, has quickly grown to be a common element to many new home inventions. So-called 'smart technology' infiltrates the home at a more micro level. Smart doorbells and locks allow for users to not only record each visitor that approaches their home, but allows them to monitor the status of each lock in their house from anywhere. Even lightbulbs have been reimagined to be 'smart,' including features like the ability to control them from one's smartphone or being able to change the light's color with the flick of a finger. The proliferation of smart-home appliances aims to service people in ways that have never been seen before.

Home automation, while sometimes written off as 'gimmicky,' has the potential to create more useful home environments for elderly people and those with special needs or reduced mobility. An individual who requires a wheelchair to move about their house can control their lights and thermostat through applications on their smartphone. People concerned for their aging family members can monitor them through security systems and can make sure that their doors are properly locked without having to directly go to check. Voice-assisted technology, seen in products like the Google Home or Amazon Alexa, provides a new sense of intimacy to the world of home automation. With voice-assistant software, users can search the internet, control music or lights, send messages, and call loved ones all by simply calling out to the device. While privacy is a common concern with these technologies and they have been proven easy to hack, the benefits of this type of technology are quite significant for the aforementioned groups of individuals. This trend in bringing ubiquitous technology into the domestic sphere is marketable for companies but also provides tangible help to people who truly could benefit from it.

SMART AND SUSTAINABLE

Home automation provides new ways in which existing structures can be rewired to reduce their carbon footprint. Sensors are able to monitor energy usage within homes and identify ways in which reductions can be made. Furthermore, home energy systems can be aided with power-generating technology that also possesses 'smart' elements. Solar panels that track the movement of the sun to ensure the highest amount of solar gain are now available to the average consumer. Sensors tracking movement can trigger lights to turn off automatically if they detect that there is no one in the room. Automation of activities to reduce the carbon footprint is a great way to motivate people to purchase these new technologies because homeowners are able to save the environment and money on their utility bills. As global warming continues to impact how people live their daily lives, it is important to develop technology aimed at engraining environmental consciousness into every area where a tangible difference can be made.

FUTURE HOME FEATURES:

LIVING SCREEN HOUSE

→ Automated systems
→ Solar panels
→ Water collection and reuse

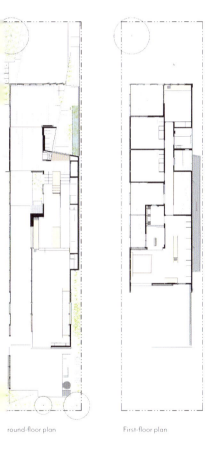

Ground-floor plan   First-floor plan

Home automation will not slow down anytime soon. Architects designing new homes commonly will work with home automation experts to ensure their designs can be equipped with these technologies either now or in the future. Home automation technology provides users with a more intimate way to live in their own homes. Their home will directly follow the commands set forth by the individual. While many people fear home automation over privacy concerns, there are many benefits to this type of technology that must be considered before completely writing it off.

Including features of home automation to support a dwelling's sustainable design is a worthwhile strategy. Such was the approach to the design of **Living Screen House** by CplusC Architectural Workshop.

Located in the North Bondi seafront community, a suburb of Sydney, Australia, the design earned many accolades and awards including a Good Design Award 2018 and short listing in the prestigious World Architectural Festival (WAF).

The 2,368-square-foot (220-square-meter) home was conceived as a private retreat for a family of five on a relatively narrow lot. The layout divides the overall area into social and family spaces. The lower level houses the kitchen, living, dining, a lap pool with glass walls, and outdoor spaces. The open plan of this level facilitates a visual connection between these spaces.

The upper floor is where the secluded private functions are located. On that floor are three bedrooms and a master bedroom with a dressing space. The designers directed views from these bedrooms to either the outdoors or the lower floor.

A notable feature of the design includes self-maintained LED-lit green living wall screens. Those screens, after which the home was named, create a unique visible effect upon arrival and entry. Special attention was also paid to additional sustainable aspects such as passive solar design which saves on energy use and costs. The openness of the building's envelope lets in natural daylight, an objective originally set by the architects. A large 10 KWh solar system is located on the roof and provides the dwelling's energy needs.

Other sustainable elements include a choice of low embodied energy building materials. In this regard some of the materials selected were recycled from the building that originally stood on the property. In addition, large rainwater storage tanks were installed.

One of the notable design features is the façade. Made of a wooden grid with windows and perforated metal panels, it lets in light and offers a growing surface for the living wall screens.

The design of Living Screen House is an excellent example of a beautiful dwelling that keeps its airiness and at the same time uses many of its design features to make it sustainable.

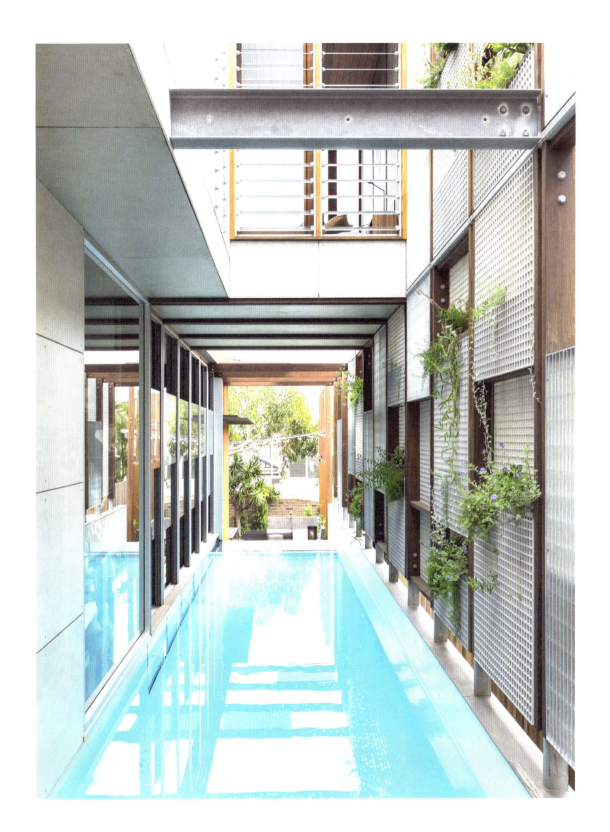

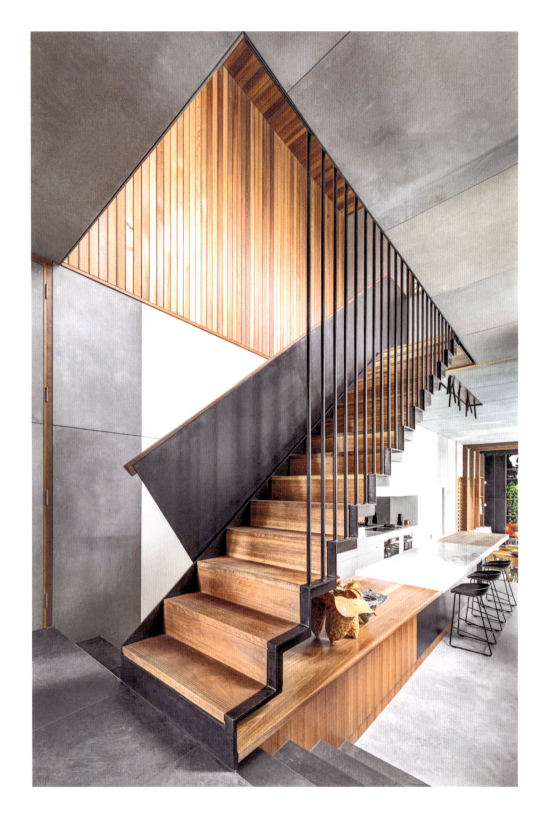

FUTURE HOME FEATURES:

BS HOUSE

→ Automated systems
→ Solar panels
→ Local materials
→ Natural heating and cooling

A design inspired by traditional homes was combined with smart-home technology in **BS House**, designed by architecture firm Reisarchitettura in 2017 for a couple that chose a site in the countryside of Puglia, Italy. The house functions both as a working studio and a relaxing retreat for the couple.

The site sits high, with a generous view over the surrounding landscape. The house is organized around a central courtyard facing the north. As the massing of the house blocks direct sunlight, this space becomes passively cooled for enjoyable outdoor living. This spatial arrangement has been used since ancient times as protection from the harsh sun. Inside the home, the living room and workspace are to the east, while private quarters are to the west. The kitchen and dining area are in the middle, with direct access to the courtyard. A separate annex to the north provides relaxing amenities. The materiality of the home reflects traditions of Puglia. The architects used a combination of dry tone and lime plaster for the walls, with oak wood frames for openings; the design of the façades makes use of these materials in a contemporary fashion.

The clients wished to have control of their home while they were away on business trips, so a KNX automation system was integrated into the house. Not only are lighting and air conditioning remotely adjustable, the system also features control of the house's security system, including the entry buzzer, door lock, and alarms. Along with these elements, energy consumption management can be monitored through a smart device application. The house generates power from photovoltaic panels, which serve the home as well as a charging port for an electric car.

Reisarchitettura designed the home with convenience and comfort in mind, combining traditional methods and modern technology to make the most of the site. BS House fully embraces home automation as a tool for sustainability.

Floor plan

CONCEPT

Sun protection and privacy

Space allocation

SMART TECHNOLOGY

OUR FUTURE HOMES:
SUSTAINABLE COMMUNITIES

Designers and builders looking toward a sustainable future are increasingly working not just in the context of individual homes or even developments, but are planning ways in which whole neighborhoods and cities can become sustainable. Key to this is an increasing use of dense urban forms, along with traffic reduction methods and an increase in green spaces.

Designing for denser living will necessarily raise questions about which forms and levels of density make neighborhoods appealing and livable. Denser urban living will help reduce urban sprawl, which in turn leads to less need for private vehicles. Planners need to then consider public transit needs, and look at ways to make neighborhoods more conducive to walking and cycling.

Ecologically, socially, and economically important, green spaces are increasingly essential parts of neighborhoods, not only to expedite walking and cycling, but for the overall mental and physical health and wellbeing of residents.

Dense urban living, transportation, and green spaces are all discussed in this section, with some inspiring examples of neighborhood projects that point the way to the future of urban planning.

LIVABLE DENSER COMMUNITIES

Key aspects to consider in planning sustainable communities

Avoid planning for sprawl

Denser urban form

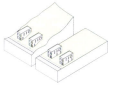

Consider existing topography

Links to neighboring communities

Multi-unit dwellings

Mixed-use zoning

Reducing urban sprawl and planning more dense urban forms will become vital to achieving sustainable neighborhoods. When large numbers of people reside in a community, a wide range of services such as public transit and commercial amenities become economically viable and possible to introduce. This in turn reduces reliance on private vehicles and makes the neighborhood walkable. The challenge is to choose an appropriate density and urban form to make these places appealing and livable.

RETHINKING URBAN DENSITY

Once the location of a neighborhood has been chosen, and its edges drawn, choosing a desired form and density will follow. Several factors determine what would be considered low-, medium-, or high-density neighborhoods: choices made with respect to the average dwelling size, type of parking, and the amount of private outdoor space will all affect the resulting densities. For example, attached units can be mixed with detached houses to elevate the overall density and limit sprawl. The attached dwellings can provide owners with privacy and affordability, and help foster a sense of place.

Single-family detached dwellings on their typically low density of four to six units per acre (10 to 15 units per hectare) are not sustainable. These homes are known to accommodate 25 percent fewer people, and consume 15 percent to 67 percent more energy than row houses or apartments. The increase in smaller and single-parent households, and an aging population, mean that detached houses once built for nuclear families may no longer meet future demand. In addition, many first-time buyers cannot afford to buy a home due to lower income. From a development perspective, dense designs such as town houses require less investment in infrastructure and produce more units per land area.

DESIGNING DENSER COMMUNITIES

For any residential development to be feasible, it must appeal to potential homebuyers. In other words, be it a low- or high-density development, the design must be attractive and livable. Therefore, the introduction and success of higher-density housing prototypes will depend on design factors that are carefully thought out to create a place where people enjoy their environment.

The planning of communities with high-density dwellings needs to be undertaken with caution. The advantageous aspects of single-family homes, such as privacy and open space, must be incorporated in new designs. Simultaneous elimination of environmentally unsustainable elements such as excessive road coverage must also be considered.

In general, urban density is a subjective term that relates to a location and culture. An Asian neighborhood is likely to be much denser than its North American counterpart, for example. The question is, therefore, how should density be regarded and what should be the common yardsticks of such neighborhoods?

HOUSING FOR SENIORS

In the coming decades, the proportion of senior citizens in many nations is projected to increase more rapidly than any other age bracket, and the time of guaranteed placement in assisted living institutions, once common in developed countries, has passed. Multigenerational living arrangements promote a sustainable lifestyle from both a social and economic perspective. Elderly persons who live alongside their offspring have the opportunity to maintain an active autonomous or semi-autonomous routine, while the younger generation provides emotional security and physical assistance when needed. Several arrangements are commonly associated with multigenerational housing.

→ Side-by-side units follow the same form as semi-detached houses and town houses where both units have the same level access yet they are separated by a partition wall. The spatial relationship between the two main entrances and the removal of certain interior partitions can create communal spaces.

→ Superimposed units are defined by level changes. While one unit has lower-level entry, the second can be accessed from an interior or exterior stairway. The elder generation often occupies the lower-level floor due to its increased accessibility.

Consideration of the site's environmental conditions needs to be a basic step in sustainable planning

1 Wind direction
2 Existing trees
3 Sun path

FUTURE HOME FEATURES:
DUJARDIN MEWS

→ Low-rise, high-density housing
→ Encourages pedestrian connections
→ Sustainable approaches including SUDs, photovoltaics and biodiverse landscaping
→ Natural light and ventilation within homes

Rooftop plan

Second-floor plan

First-floor plan

Ground-floor plan

By combining planning features from low-density and high-density designs one can introduce urban forms with a unique character. Such design averages 25 units per acre (55 units per hectare), with rear private parking and yards for each unit. Minimal, though acceptable, widths separate the houses. Moreover, green open space located at the center of the cluster can be made accessible from each unit, which is associated with the notion that public parks are crucial to community interaction.

In 2017 a former industrial site was transformed into a pedestrian-friendly neighborhood at **Dujardin Mews**, a council-led social housing development in London, UK, designed by Karakusevic Carson Architects in collaboration with Maccreanor Lavington Architects. The project, in Enfield, consists of one- to four-bedroom homes to cater for individuals and families of different sizes.

The site is located on remediated brownfield land—where any potential contaminants have been removed—that was previously inaccessible. The development creates a central pedestrian 'homezone' route that runs through the site, forming a new north–south connection to the main road. An apartment block to the south acts as a buffer to industrial buildings and forms a turning corner leading to the pedestrian street. The main entrances of the houses all face the street. The row of town houses to the west are mainly two stories in height, blending in with the profiles of the neighboring development, while those on the east side are three-story.

The town houses that make up much of the social housing part of the project are designed in a way to maximise density on the site without sacrificing a domestic scale. A feeling of community is maintained by promoting passive surveillance for safety and facilitating social connections between neighbors through the arrangement of private entrances and balconies that line the central pedestrian route. The arrangement of homes in terraces reduces construction and energy costs due to the shared wall between each unit. Some roofs are biodiverse and some feature solar panels, to contribute to a greener neighborhood. A Sustainable Urban Drainage System (SUDS) belowground controls rainwater runoff.

Dujardin Mews features different roof profiles that provide diversity to the street façades, while optimizing daylight into the public realm. The material palette is primarily brick, referencing the typical London street; relief details in the brick layout add character and visual variety. The homes all have large floor-to-ceiling heights with substantial windows that provides much natural light and ventilation. Homes bordering the school to the north have enclosed backyards for more privacy; sheltered first-floor terraces on these homes create private outdoor space facing the street to avoid overlooking onto the neighboring school and providing natural surveillance to the streetscape. Parking is located along both sides of the street close to the entrances of people's homes.

The architects combine an original interpretation of a traditional terraced street with sustainable approaches to create a low-energy and high-quality community of homes. The connections made inside the neighborhood and with its surrounding context make it a good model for housing design on a constrained site.

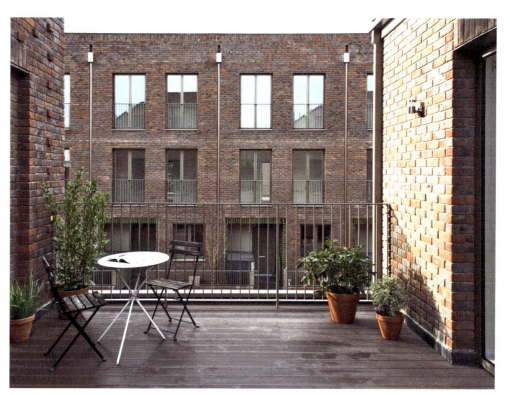

LIVABLE DENSER COMMUNITIES

FUTURE HOME FEATURES:

ST. CHAD'S

→ Dense housing
→ Encourages physical activity
→ Green spaces
→ Integration of old and new

Second-floor plan

First-floor plan

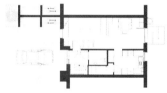
Ground-floor plan

Creating a livable community was also the aim of Bell Phillips Architects, who designed **St. Chad's** in Essex, UK, in 2017. Located near low-density housing and docks for industrial activity, the site that St. Chad's stands on was previously an underused area of Tilbury. The local council noted that the site had potential, and enlisted Bell Phillips Architects to transform it into the vibrant community it is today. The project provides much-needed affordable housing in the form of two- to three-story town houses.

As the location was not a well-established part of the town, it did not have a strong character. The architects strived to give the community a sense of place. Streets in the community connect to the existing street layout, forming linear grid patterns. A diagonal grid intersects this, with one avenue converted to a long park. It was designed to have an abundance of plants, enhancing biodiversity and enriching the landscape. In doing so, it became an inviting space for the community to enjoy nature, promoting a healthy lifestyle. This linear park leads to a junction point of green spaces, where the residents can meet and socialize. Each town house also has its own private garden, where homeowners can grow their own food.

The houses line up to create lanes of terrace housing. Although they may look homogenous from afar, at a closer look it is apparent that the architects played with the façades and roofs for a whimsical feeling, making the most from the limited material palette of two brick types. Neighboring houses have the same spatial layout, but different colored brick makes each of them stand out, along with roofs that vary in slope. Some town houses have two stories, while others on the same block may have three. All these characteristics make the neighborhood interesting, adding character and a sense of place to the streets.

The architects of St. Chad's were able to revitalize the area into a healthy, livable community. The planning of the project also demonstrates another aspect that is bound to be the way of the future: integration of new and old. Through the street planning and design details, St. Chad's has become an engaging place to be, bringing life into the neighborhood.

The success of developments like Dujardin Mews and St. Chad's make it clear that, despite some legal and market barriers to dense residential designs, those challenges can be overcome. Issues involving circulation and parking, private and public open space provisions, and individual and community identity can all be thoughtfully addressed to attract residents who are looking for quality livable accommodations while at the same time reducing overall energy consumption and pollution.

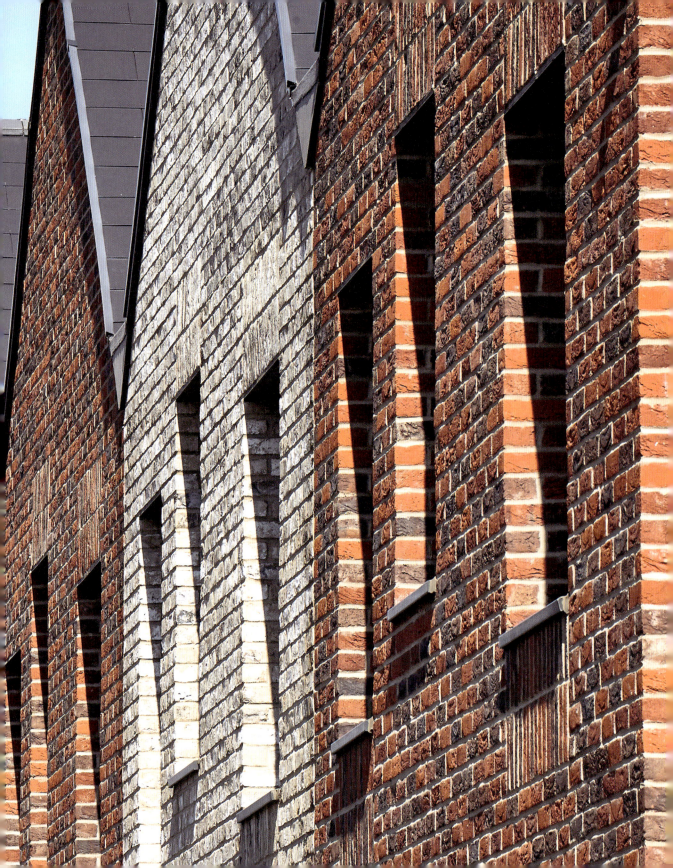

LIVABLE DENSER COMMUNITIES

COMMUNITIES ON THE MOVE

Speed reduction measures for vehicles that ensure safety of pedestrians and, as a result, more walkability

1. Narrow entry to street
2. Identify street crossing
3. Change level and texture of intersection
4. Sidewalk projection
5. Short block
6. Narrow street
7. Bike path
8. Shared street

Measures that contribute to a wider use of public transit

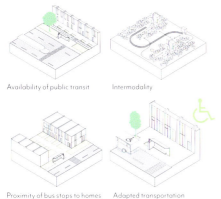

Availability of public transit
Intermodality
Proximity of bus stops to homes
Adapted transportation
Bus shelters
Display of bus schedules

Bike rental stations

Bicycles on bus

Automobile usage and its supporting infrastructure—including parking lots, paved streets, and sidewalks—increase greenhouse gas emissions and urban heat. Walkable neighborhoods are a sustainable solution and have power to improve the quality of life and health of residents. A range of trends and measures have demonstrated how communities can reduce traffic and rely instead on active mobility by foot or bicycle.

CAR-FREE ENVIRONMENTS

Many of the trips taken daily by drivers are to non-residential destinations and could be avoided altogether if these functions were closer to home. Perhaps the most obvious solution is for key neighborhood amenities to be placed in strategic locations and clustered to make it easy to visit several destinations in a single trip.

Public transit is another important element to consider in the development of local mobility networks. Most municipalities argue that such systems need to be economically self-sustaining, an objective that is hard to achieve without substantial ridership. Cost-saving measures may include smaller buses that use alternative sources of energy like those currently used in many European cities. Offering services on demand might increase convenience and efficiency. Another important consideration: special vehicles might be provided for seniors and others with reduced mobility.

Of course, sustainable planners cannot replace the automobile with public transit alone—active transportation must be enabled, too. Therefore, the planners of car-free communities not only deprioritize cars, but also work to put pedestrians, cyclists, and children at play first. For example, in the Netherlands some streets are called woonerf, meaning 'streets for living.' These streets are shared between pedestrians, bicycles, transit vehicles, and automobiles, all with no distinction between sidewalks and car lanes. The woonerf rely on narrow streets and gentle curves to slow traffic and create a safer environment for pedestrians and cyclists. Streets with a width of 20 feet (6 meters) have been observed to accommodate both pedestrians and drivers since, again, the cars move slowly, allowing pedestrians to feel at ease.

WALKING AND CYCLING

Over the past decade, there has been a large increase in the funding of pro-bike policies and initiatives by governments and municipalities. In high-density developments the relatively limited area that neighborhoods occupy and the fewer vehicles that travel on their roads make them highly suitable for active modes of mobility.

Well-marked paths, signage, traffic calming devices, and road markings, tend to foster biking and walking. Such strategies were introduced by Dutch, Danish, and German cities to support cycling. Those strategies included: bike-parking facilities, coordination with public transportation, traffic education and training, and the enactment of supporting traffic laws. To promote cycling the same districts offered convenient access to bikes through sharing programs, bike-trip planning, and public-awareness campaigns. Driving was discouraged by reducing automobile speed limits, increasing parking charges, automobile taxation, and strict land-use policies.

WATCH WHERE YOU PARK!

The careful placement of parking spaces is one way to discourage the use of cars. Parking spaces made of pavement absorb heat and collect water on the surface, not allowing the soil below to filter the rainwater. Those parking areas should serve more than one function and be integrated into the landscape. Another alternative is off-street parking composed of permeable paving material. Grouped parking spaces also offer residents financial savings. A space that accommodates about 20 cars is recommended to maximize flexibility in arrangement of space, minimize construction and maintenance costs, and reduce negative impact on surrounding buildings.

FUTURE HOME FEATURES:
HAMMARBY SJÖSTAD

→ Dense neighborhood
→ Reycling and reuse
→ Physical activity promoted
→ Green spaces
→ Energy-efficient buildings

Accommodating pedestrians can also be achieved by introducing safety-awareness programs. These include simple and relatively inexpensive educational interventions aimed at increasing the awareness walkers and motorists have of each another's presence. Other measures with a higher price-tag can be introduced in denser areas that are known to be more walkable: road bumps can reduce speeds, or highly textured driving surfaces can be used. The bumps can be placed at the entrance to a street to indicate an increase in residential density and the need to slow down. Stamped concrete or cobblestone segments can also be effective while adding emphasis to gateways and entrances. A technique that is particularly useful when dealing with heavily traveled streets is to raise the level of the road at intersections. As a result, the continuous and uninterrupted crosswalk ensures that pedestrians have priority. These measures will contribute to making a community pedestrian and cyclist friendly.

Providing and encouraging alternative methods of transportation is at the heart of **Hammarby Sjöstad**, a development planned and built in Stockholm, Sweden, between 2013 and 2018 with the masterplan designed by White Arkitekter. The green community was created from a previously dilapidated industrial waste site as part of an urban regeneration project headed by the Swedish government in collaboration with land developers. The district was completely overhauled by incorporating environmental technologies, and providing green public spaces and convenient public transportation to engage the community in a sustainable urban lifestyle.

The creation of a circular economy was a key part in the development of Hammarby Sjöstad. In the construction process, waste was kept to a minimum and efficient use of resources was ensured. Since material, transportation, and manufacturing methods all contribute to the carbon footprint, careful choices were made to minimize carbon dioxide emissions. The infrastructure system was designed to be a closed loop, with reuse of water, energy, and waste to reduce the amount of resources going into the system. Wastewater is treated locally, and reused for industrial and agricultural purposes. In the treatment process, biogas is created; this byproduct is then used as fuel for modes of public transportation.

The success of Hammarby Sjöstad in becoming a car-free environment stems from the availability of alternate transportation, and the cooperation of parties developing the land. Real-estate developers, in their projects in Hammarby Sjöstad, limited the amount of parking space available for residents. Community wide, there is an average of 0.7 spaces per dwelling; use of electric cars is promoted with the installation of 500 charging points. The density of the site also facilitates walking and cycling, since commercial areas and amenities are located at closer distances than in suburban developments. Elements of the project are optimized for pedestrian use, such as the wide, landscaped sidewalks, and various green spaces.

Despite the large scale of Hammarby Sjöstad, sustainable and energy-efficient living was achieved through the collaborative efforts of the government and the community. There are many takeaways from it; the circular economy and the effective methods of encouraging a car-free lifestyle can be applied to projects of a smaller scale that are bound to be a way of the future.

Floor plan 538 ft² (50 m²)

Floor plan 850 ft² (79 m²)

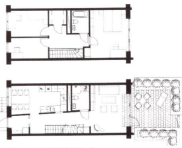

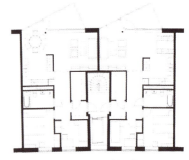
Floor plan 1,076 ft² (100 m²)

Floor plan per dwelling 850 ft² (79 m²)

COMMUNITIES ON THE MOVE

Significant amounts of space dedicated to pedestrians and cyclist combine with affordable housing, owner-occupied housing, small-scale businesses, and a sporting facility in **Villa Industria**, a residential project in Hilversum, the Netherlands. In 2018, architecture firm Mecanoo converted the former industrial site into a pedestrian- and bike-friendly community that prioritizes public space for its residents.

Prior to the construction of Villa Industria, the area existed as a gap breaking the flow of the city. The addition of this community re-integrates the site back into the urban fabric, connecting the communities around it. The land is divided into small sections, each containing different types of housing and other buildings, to bring the development from an industrial scale to a human scale. One area contains three distinct apartment buildings that reference the gasometers that were on the site previously; another contains smaller apartment buildings, connected to the athletics center and businesses; others contain town houses of different forms, organized in back-to-back and courtyard formations to generate smaller communities within a large one. All town-house blocks were designed with different details in the brickwork façade, incorporating variety within an overall visually coherent project.

Villa Industria was designed with the intention of providing substantial public space for pedestrians and cyclists. To do so, traffic was redirected belowground; recessed parking is present throughout the site, with a road running underground where railroad tracks were previously located. Ground openings allow light and air through to the lower level while providing a connection with the spaces above. The apartments nearby are surrounded by park area leading to pedestrian streets, which all convene at a central park area that is easily accessible for residents and visitors. Two of the town-house divisions form triangular courtyards that facilitate interactions between neighbors, while another division has homes situated in rows that each open onto pedestrian streets. All town houses include gardens, a semi-public space defined by hedges that provides residents an opportunity to personalize their environment and at the same time acts as a transition area between public and private.

The abundance and allocation of Villa Industria's green spaces pr(active living among its residents. Cars are secondary to pedestrian and housing is brought back to a comfortable human scale.

FUTURE HOME FEATURES:
VILLA INDUSTRIA

→ Dense neighborhood
→ Physical activity promoted
→ Green spaces
→ Pedestrian streets

FUTURE HOMES

OPEN SPACES

Urban aspects of sustainable communities

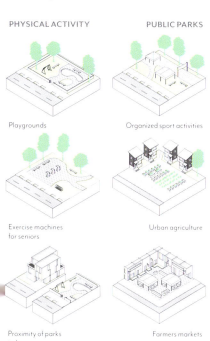

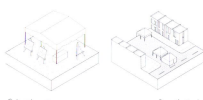

Open spaces are essential to quality of life for a neighborhood's residents. Their contribution to human physical and mental health has been considered vital for centuries: exposure to natural areas was once used to treat diseases brought on by the poor urban hygiene of days past. Today, while cities in developed nations no longer suffer from these poor sanitary conditions, the health benefits of green space remain—and we have a better understanding of their ecological, social, and economic importance. These spaces are a more essential element of the neighborhood than ever, given the present shift toward greater density.

Green areas improve a community's sustainability in many ways; for one, they mitigate the 'urban heat island' effect that contributes to summer peak energy demands, air-conditioning costs, air pollution, greenhouse gas emissions, heat-related illness, and decreased water quality.

Another way in which open areas contribute to neighborhood sustainability is in their encouragement of an active lifestyle. Public health, planning, and community design are closely linked, and a sustainable community with green spaces can help tackle health inequalities, from obesity to mental health. Well-planned neighborhoods with high pedestrian activity and bike riding reduce automobile usage.

A continuous landscape of greenery helps preserve the biodiversity of an area, allowing various species to survive and circulate much as they do in wilder spaces. Continuity of such open space can be difficult to accomplish in high-density developments but is achievable if corridors of greenery are combined with walkways to link urban green patches to big parks outside the community.

Open spaces confer significant psychological benefits. Green areas can counter the effects of crowding in high-density housing environments. The availability of green space empowers people, ensuring they no longer feel confined in small apartments, but instead can dramatically change their surroundings at will.

PLANNING FOR LIVABILITY

Open spaces need to be planned in accord with residents' variable lifestyles and life stages. A divide between areas for intimate versus lively activity should be physically represented in the space. Vegetation can act as a buffer between passive sections, for leisurely picnics and reading, and active areas, for walking and biking. Passive sections are better suited to contained areas far from roads.

School-age children require many facilities to host a range of activities, and the distribution of open space for this function will vary between neighborhoods depending on each community's demographic profile. Green areas within a development can be designed so that the space and homes involved work in conjunction to provide children with better supervision and thus safety.

When areas for community gardens are provided, they can be private, shared, or both. Shared garden lots should have a water supply system and a storage area for tools. Rooftop gardens can be considered when ground space is otherwise occupied.

Different methods of landscape design can be used to establish those ratios. Conservation design calls for the maintenance of the original landscape by designing buildings around nature, as opposed to leveling an entire site. Although initial land costs might be elevated, landscaping and design expenses are reduced. An alternative method to create multifunction open spaces in an urban context is the use of paved areas, like parking lots and pedestrian streets.

The front yard is important as it is a transition zone between the home's private and public realms. It links residents to the neighborhood in providing opportunity for social interaction, but still operates as a buffer zone, giving occupants privacy. Even when the building is 'pushed' forward to accommodate a larger backyard space, the identity of the front yard can be maintained with landscaping or fencing. The demarcation provided by the home's entrance can be achieved with a step, a porch, or other selected detailing. When private open space in the front is limited, balconies can provide valuable outdoor areas.

An example of planning that incorporates new and retained green spaces is **Bryant Heights**, built in an already established neighborhood of Seattle in Washington, USA. The development combines different housing and program types with a focus on green spaces to merge higher-density living with the mid-density residential district. It consists of town houses, single-family homes, condominiums, and live/work lofts, as well as commercial space. Built by Johnston Architects, it was completed in 2018.

Bryant Heights takes up a street block previously occupied by a hospital campus; its development reintegrates the site back into the urban fabric. To the north, east, and west are residential blocks, while to the south is a busy local commercial street. To blend with the dynamic of the neighborhood, the architects proposed a gradient of building density with commercial space, live/work, and condominiums in the south to single-family homes in the north. Topography changes were incorporated within the development to break up the large scale, also resulting in an interesting pedestrian experience. Town houses at Bryant Heights connect up to three units, economizing space while giving most units the privacy of a semi-detached home. All town-house blocks were designed with different façades to avoid visual monotony while having a more bespoke feeling. The row of mixed-use commercial properties and condominiums maintain the pedestrian flow of the street, keeping it active.

In the development, houses neighboring the streets are equipped with large front yards, often with retained trees, providing more privacy. Town houses also have large front yards, providing homeowners with their own garden and contributing to the overall greenscape of the development. The preservation of existing trees also gives a sense of permanence to the homes, while maintaining biodiversity on the site. Two retained oak trees shape the central path within the neighborhood that connects the town houses. Combined with other pedestrian paths throughout the development, they blend the different density zones into one cohesive community. Native plants were grown as part of the landscape design, cutting down maintenance costs and minimizing disturbance to the environment.

FUTURE HOME FEATURES:
BRYANT HEIGHTS

→ **High-density living**
→ **Physical activity promoted**
→ **Green spaces and native plants**
→ **Biodiversity**

OPEN SPACES

OPEN SPACES

Co-housing developments have become increasingly prevalent in cities throughout the UK. In these neighborhoods, in addition to their individuals homes the residents share a community social space. The homeowners have joint ownership of common spaces, which is managed by the residents themselves. Co-housing schemes bring together people who care about the environment, allowing the community to work toward a single greener goal.

Marmalade Lane designed by Mole Architects is a co-housing development in Cambridge, UK. It contains four modular dwelling types that are distributed on the site flexibly, from one-bedroom apartments to four-bedroom homes to accommodate people of all backgrounds. The development features customization of both the interior and exterior of the homes, giving homeowners the ability to personalize their houses according to their needs and lifestyles. This also prevents visual monotony in the community. The homes are designed according to passive principles, with 9.65-inch-thick (245-millimeter-thick) insulation in the walls and triple-glazed windows. A Swedish prefabricated timber panel system was used in construction, with an airtightness of less than 3m3/hr/m2@50PPa. Photovoltaic panels on the roofs of all buildings contribute to the energy use of the neighborhood; the calculated space heating demand of the houses averaged 35kWhr/m2/yr.

The community was designed to emphasize a socially active, eco-friendly lifestyle. The Shared Garden acts as the center of the neighborhood block, taking up the most area. It contains green space for activities of people of all ages. Children can play, adults can socialize, and a dedicated garden is available for all residents to grow their own food. This area features rainwater management as well as retained trees from before the development of Marmalade Lane, integrating the development into the existing environment. Two rows of homes border the Shared Garden, each with their own yards. An additional row of town houses sits beside the main road, connected to the neighborhood with a green laneway. The sequence of spaces becomes increasingly private approaching the garden; parking spaces are located at the periphery of the neighborhood, ensuring a safe playing space for children inside the community and to promote a car-free lifestyle for all.

The green features of Marmalade Lane as well as the customization of its homes creates an environment that is personalized for all, bringing together a community that works together toward a more sustainable social future.

The planning and provision of open spaces in higher-density housing developments like Bryant Heights and Marmalade Lane require much care and thought. Private outdoor space, whether in the form of front or back yards, patios, decks, balconies, or roof terraces, must be provided along with public outdoor space, which can be implemented in a variety of patterns. Additionally, the design of the landscape itself, including engineered features and vegetation, should be functional and aesthetically appealing to create an inviting environment.

FUTURE HOME FEATURES:
MARMALADE LANE
➜ **Green spaces**
➜ **Natural light and ventilation**
➜ **Solar heating**

ACKNOWLEDGMENTS

Innovative residential design was a topic of my research and practice for years. Over that time, I explored and introduced new ideas in the planning of homes and communities and oversaw construction of housing prototypes. The work included collaboration with numerous colleagues, funders, assistants, and students who directly and indirectly inspired the generation of the ideas and the writing of this book. My apology if I have mistakenly omitted the name of someone who contributed to the ideas or the text of this book. I will do my best to correct an omission in future editions.

Isabella Rubial Carvajal and Charles Gregoire were instrumental in contributing to the designs expressed here and the generation of most of the illustrations that accompany the chapters. Their contribution and work over the years is most appreciated.

Thanks to Diana Nigmatullina and Nathalie Marj for drawing many of the illustrations for this book with utmost dedication and attention to detail and accuracy. Gratitude also to Jin j. Zhao and Zhong Cai for their drawings. Thanks to Brian McGinn for his contribution to the chapter on home automation and for editing the text.

Jiahui (Cindy) Duan played a key role in finding the outstanding projects listed here and describing them. Her dedication, eye for good design, hard work, and interest in the subject are appreciated.

I would like to express my gratitude to the management and editorial team at Images Publishing with whom I collaborated for several years for ushering the book in and for their patience and guidance in seeing it through. Many thanks also go to Kate James for the outstanding editing and the structuring of the text.

Thanks to the McGill University's School of Architecture where the genesis of the ideas expressed here began and my own research was carried out.

Finally, my heartfelt thanks and appreciation to my wife Sorel Friedman, PhD, and children Paloma and Ben for their love and support.

CONTRIBUTING FIRMS

My thanks go to the following firms who generously allowed me to include their work.

AGo Architects
Aline Architect
Arthur Casas
Austin Maynard Architects
Batay-Csorba Architects
Bell Phillips Architects
Benn & Penna Architecture
CplusC Architectural Workshop
DKO Architecture and SLAB
Dravitzki Brown
Estudio Borrachia
Geraghty Taylor
Interface Studio Architects (ISA)
J_spy Architecture
John Wardle Architects
Johnston Architects
Karakusevic Carson Architects with Maccreanor Lavington Architects
Mecanoo
Mole Architects
Pearl Homes
Reisarchitettura
Ross Street Design
Studio Architectuur MAKEN
TDO
Tegnestuen LOKAL
Tenhachi Architect & Interior Design
Urban Rural Systems
White Arkitekter
Zero Studio

APPENDIX

BIBLIOGRAPHY

CHAPTER 1: GREEN MATERIALS

De Gouverneur
Budds, Diana. 'This Dutch Company Turns Demolished Buildings Into Beautiful Materials.' *Fast Company*, October 26, 2016. Accessed February 6, 2019. www.fastcompany.com/3064915/this-dutch-company-turns-demolished-buildings-into-beautiful-materials

'De Gouverneur / Architectuur MAKEN.' *Archdaily*, October 1, 2016. Accessed February 6, 2019. www.archdaily.com/796180/de-gouverneur-architectuur-maken

Gould, Hannah. 'The Rotterdam couple that will live in a house made from waste.' *The Guardian*, May 21, 2016. Accessed February 6, 2019. www.theguardian.com/sustainable-business/2016/may/21/rotterdam-couple-house-made-from-waste-stonecycling-bricks-netherlands

TK-33
'Danish home champions wood over concrete for lower carbon emissions.' *Inhabitat*. Accessed January 26, 2019. www.inhabitat.com/danish-home-champions-wood-over-concrete-for-lower-carbon-emissions

'TK-33 / Tegnestuen LOKAL.' *Archdaily*. Accessed January 26, 2019. www.archdaily.com/906288/tk-33-tegnestuen-lokal

CHAPTER 2: AFFORDABILITY

Expandable House
'Expandable House / Urban Rural Systems.' *Archdaily*, April 3, 2018. Accessed February 7, 2019. www.archdaily.com/891811/expandable-house-urban-rural-systems

'Rumah Tambah.' *ur-scape*. Accessed February 7, 2019. www.urs.fcl.sg/category/rumah-tambah (site inactive at time of publication)

Mausam–House of the Seasons
'Mausam–House of the Seasons / ZERO STUDIO.' *Archdaily*, October 10, 2017. Accessed February 9, 2019. www.archdaily.com/881297/mausam-house-of-the-seasons-zero-studio

CHAPTER 3: INNOVATIVE CONSTRUCTION

FAB House
'FAB House — TDO.' *TDO Architecture*. Accessed September 2, 2022. www.tdoarchitecture.com/fab-house/yn5fb48zgxphk52l23jqans9dbkpvn

Griffiths, Alyn. 'TV presenter George Clarke and TDO unveil terrace of prefabricated Fab Houses.' *dezeen*, April 30, 2018. Accessed September 2, 2022. www.dezeen.com/2018/04/30/tv-presenter-george-clarke-tdo-prefabricated-fab-houses

Wilson, Rob. 'Fab Gear', *Architects' Journal* (April 12, 2018): 36–47.

SysHaus
Kim, Sheila. 'Brazilian Prefab by Studio Arthur Casas.' *Architectural Record* 206, no. 9 (2018). Accessed September 2, 2022. www.architecturalrecord.com/articles/13620-brazilian-prefab-by-studio-arthur-casas

Larvas, Nick. 'Sustainable flatpack SysHaus pops up in less than a month.' *New Atlas*, August 30, 2018. Accessed September 2, 2022. www.newatlas.com/flatpack-sustainable-syshaus-prefab/56157

'SysHaus.' *Studio Arthur Casas*. Accessed September 2, 2022. www.arthurcasas.com/projects/syshaus

CHAPTER 4: DESIGNING EXTERIORS

Đại Kim House
'Đại Kim house / Aline Architect.' *Archdaily*, December 8, 2018. Accessed February 8, 2019. www.archdaily.com/907278/dai-kim-house-aline-architect

Double Duplex
'Double Duplex.' *Batay-Csorba Architects*. Accessed February 4, 2019. www.batay-csorba.com/2683068-double-duplex#1

'Double Duplex / Batay-Csorba Architects.' *Archdaily*, April 25, 2017. Accessed February 4, 2019. www.archdaily.com/869886/double-duplex-batay-csorba-architects

CHAPTER 5: CREATIVE DESIGNS

Powerhouse
'Powerhouse - ISA'. *ISA*. Accessed January 30, 2019. www.is-architects.com/powerhouse

'Powerhouse - ISA'. *Archdaily*, December 24, 2016. Accessed January 30, 2019. www.archdaily.com/801443/powerhouse-isa

Woodview Mews
'Livinhome / Woodview Mews | Geraghty Taylor.' *Geraghty Taylor*. Accessed January 28, 2019. www.geraghtytaylor.com/project/livinhome-woodview-mews (site inactive at time of publication)

'Woodview Mews / Geraghty Taylor Architects.' *Archdaily*, July 14, 2015. Accessed January 28, 2019. www.archdaily.com/769804/woodview-mews-geraghty-taylor-architects

'Woodview Mews by Geraghty Taylor Architects.' *Architonic*. Accessed January 28, 2019. www.architonic.com/en/project/geraghty-taylor-architects-woodview-mews/5102858

CHAPTER 6: XERISCAPED GARDENS

Ross Street House

'The Ross Street House by Richard Wittschiebe Hand Architects.' *Contemporist*. Accessed January 26, 2021. www.contemporist.com/2010/02/25/the-ross-street-house-by-richard-wittschiebe-hand-architects/

Wong, Kenneth. 'When it Comes to LEED, Platinum is the New Green.' *Cadalyst*. Accessed January 26, 2021. www.cadalyst.com/aec/when-it-comes-leed-platinum-new-green-13014

CHAPTER 7: ADAPTABLE INTERIORS

Campbell Street

'Campbell Street.' *DKO*. Accessed February 3, 2019. www.dko.com.au/project/campbell-street

'Campbell Street / DKO Architecture + SLAB.' *Archdaily*, January 6, 2019. Accessed February 3, 2019. www.archdaily.com/908935/campbell-street-dko-architecture-plus-slab

Mousa, David. 'Urban Insider Episode One: 120 Campbell St, Collingwood by Milieu.' *The Urban Developer*, October 12, 2017. Accessed February 3, 2019. www.theurbandeveloper.com/articles/urban-insider-episode-one-120-campbell-st-collingwood-milieu

Smith, James Lyall. 'Campbell Street.' *The Local Project*, May 18, 2018. Accessed February 3, 2019. www.thelocalproject.com.au/campbell-street-by-milieu-property-project-archive-collingwood-vic-australia

Whittaker Cube

Norris, Brodie. 'A Smaller Home Allows for Immaculate Details and Rich Materials.' *Lunchbox Architect*. Accessed February 6, 2019. www.lunchboxarchitect.com/featured/the-whittaker-cube-dravitzki-brown

'The Whittaker Cube / Dravitzki & Brown.' *Archdaily*, October 12, 2016. Accessed February 6, 2019. www.archdaily.com/797149/the-whittaker-cube-dravitzki-and-brown

CHAPTER 8: SMART STORAGE

3500 Millimetre House

'3500 Millimetre House / Ago Architects' *Archdaily*, January 15, 2019. Accessed February 7, 2019. www.archdaily.com/909456/3500-millimetre-house-ago-architects

Mills House

'Mills, the toy management house.' *Austin Maynard Architects*. Accessed September 2, 2022. www.maynardarchitects.com/#/053204149098

'Mills House / Austin Maynard Architects.' *Archdaily*, February 1, 2016. Accessed September 2, 2022. www.archdaily.com/781213/mills-house-andrew-maynard-architects

CHAPTER 9: FUTURE KITCHENS

Surry Hills House

'Surry Hills House / Benn & Penna Architecture.' *Archdaily*, April 3, 2017. Accessed February 9, 2019. www.archdaily.com/868294/surry-hills-house-benn-and-penna-architecture

Tenhachi House

'Tenhachi House / .8 Tenhachi Architect & Interior Design.' *Archdaily*, June 13, 2016. Accessed February 9, 2019. www.archdaily.com/789221/tenhachi-house-8-tenhachi-architect-and-interior-design

CHAPTER 10: ENERGY EFFICIENCY

Hunter's Point

Alter, Floyd. 'Florida development is a trifecta of solar power, size and efficiency.' *Treehugger*. Accessed November 12, 2018. www.treehugger.com/green-architecture/florida-development-trifecta-solar-power-size-and-efficiency.html

'First Pearl Home Community, Hunters Point, Set for Historic Cortez, Florida.' *Cision*. Accessed January 12, 2018. www.prnewswire.com/news-releases/first-pearl-home-community-hunters-point-set-for-historic-cortez-florida-300581956.html

'Our Vision— Hunter's Point.' www.hunterspointfl.com/the-vision

'Pearl Homes Details Plans for Hunters Point in Cortez, Fla.' *Builder*, January 12, 2018. Accessed January 21, 2018. www.builderonline.com/land/local-markets/pearl-homes-details-plans-for-hunters-point-in-cortez-fla_o

Limestone House

'Off the Grid.' *John Wardle Architects*. Accessed January 28, 2019. www.johnwardlearchitects.com/stories/off-the-grid

Mills, Kylie. Sime, Shanice. 'John Wardle-designed Passive House in Mt Gambier limestone.' *The Fifth Estate*, September 25, 2018. Accessed January 28, 2019. www.thefifthestate.com.au/innovation/residential-2/john-wardell-passive-house-limestone

CHAPTER 11: SUSTAINABLE UTILITIES

Catskills House

'Catskills House / J_spy Architecture and Design.' *Archdaily*, April 9, 2018. Accessed February 9, 2019. www.archdaily.com/891966/catskills-house-j-spy-architecture-and-design

Lasky, Julie. 'Two Designers Create a Small but Luxe Retreat in the Catskills.' *Dwell*, April 9, 2018. Accessed February 9, 2019. www.dwell.com/article/two-designers-create-a-small-but-luxe-retreat-in-the-catskills-953fcd77

Holmberg House

'Holmberg House / Estudio Borrachia.' *Archdaily*, May 30, 2017. Accessed February 9, 2019. www.archdaily.com/872169/holmberg-house-estudio-borrachia

CHAPTER 12: SMART TECHNOLOGY

Living Screen House

'Living Screen House / CplusC Architectural Workshop.' *Archdaily*, April 11, 2021. Accessed September 17, 2021. www.archdaily.com/870660/north-bondi-cplusc-architectural-workshop

'Living Screen House / CplusC Architectural Workshop.' *Dwell*. Accessed September 17, 2021. www.dwell.com/home/living-screen-house-a87199a5

'Living Screen House / CplusC Architectural Workshop.' *Premier*. Accessed September 17, 2021. www.premierconstructionnews.com/2018/02/06/living-screen-house/

BS House

'BS House / Reisarchitettura.' *Archdaily*, November 12, 2018. Accessed February 7, 2019. www.archdaily.com/905570/bs-house-reisarchitettura

CHAPTER 13: LIVABLE DENSER COMMUNITIES

Dujardin Mews

'Dujardin Mews.' *Arqa*, November 23, 2017. Accessed January 28, 2019. www.arqa.com/en/architecture/dujardin-mews.html

'Dujardin Mews.' *Karakusevic Carson Architects*. Accessed January 28, 2019. www.karakusevic-carson.com/work/dujardin-mews

'Dujardin Mews Walking Tour.' *Open House London 2018*. Accessed January 28, 2019. www.openhouselondon.open-city.org.uk/listings/7484 (site inactive at time of publication)

Pearman, Hugh. 'Dujardin Mews by Karakusevic Carson and MaccreanorLavington.' *Architectural Record*, October 1, 2018. Accessed January 28, 2019. www.architecturalrecord.com/articles/13662-dujardin-mews-by-karakusevic-carson-and-maccreanorlavington

St. Chad's

'St Chad's.' *RIBA*. Accessed February 9, 2019. www.architecture.com/awards-and-competitions-landing-page/awards/riba-regional-awards/riba-east-award-winners/2018/st-chads

'St. Chad's.' *Bell Phillips Architects*. Accessed February 9, 2019. www.bellphillips.com/project/st-chads/#slider-12

'St Chad's, Tilbury.' *The RIBA Journal*, May 24, 2018. Accessed February 9, 2019. www.ribaj.com/buildings/regional-awards-2018-st-chads-tilbury-bell-phillips-architects

CHAPTER 14: COMMUNITIES ON THE MOVE

Hammarby Sjöstad

'Hammarby Sjöstad regeneration.' *White Arkitekter*. Accessed February 9, 2019. www.whitearkitekter.com/project/hammarby-sjostad

'Hammarby Sjöstad, Stockholm, Sweden.' *Urban Green-Blue Grids*. Accessed February 9, 2019. www.urbangreenbluegrids.com/projects/hammarby-sjostad-stockholm-sweden

Villa Industria

Cinar, Deniz. 'Morphological Connections at the Villa Industria.' *XXI Magazine*, July 12, 2017. Accessed January 29, 2019. www.xximagazine.com/c/morphological-connections-at-the-villa-industria

'Masterplan Villa Industria.' *Mecanoo*. Accessed January 29, 2019. www.mecanoo.nl/Projects/project/182/Masterplan-Villa-Industria

Stevens, Philip. 'Mecanoo's 'Villa Industria' masterplan includes residential towers that resemble gasometers.' *Designboom*, July 10, 2018. Accessed January 29, 2019. www.designboom.com/architecture/mecanoo-villa-industria-masterplan-hilversum-netherlands-07-10-2018

CHAPTER 15: OPEN SPACES

Bryant Heights

'Bryant Heights.' *Fazio Associates*. Accessed February 5, 2019. www.fazioassociates.com/bryant-heights

'Bryant Heights.' *Johnston Architects*. Accessed February 5, 2019. www.johnstonarchitects.com/bryant-heights

Dunham, Sandy. '5 architectural approaches that are shaping the way we live.' *Seattle Times*, September 12, 2018. Accessed February 5, 2019. www.seattletimes.com/pacific-nw-magazine/5-architectural-approaches-that-are-shaping-the-way-we-live

Marmalade Lane

'Marmalade Lane, Cambridge, 2018.' *Mole Architects*. Accessed February 5, 2019. www.molearchitects.co.uk/projects/housing/k1-cambridge-co-housing

'Press Release: Marmalade Lane Under Way.' *Town*, June 28, 2017. Accessed February 5, 2019. www.wearetown.co.uk/marmalade-lane-construction-begins

PROJECT & PHOTOGRAPHY DETAILS

De Gouverneur   17–23
Studio Architectuur MAKEN | architectuurmaken.nl
Location Rotterdam, The Netherlands
Completed 2016
Photography Ossip van Duivenbode, Frank Hanswijk, Studio Architectuur MAKEN

TK-33   24–31
Tegnestuen LOKAL | tegnestuenlokal.dk
Location Tikøb, Denmark
Completed 2017
Photography Jan Ove Christensen, Peter Jørgensen

Expandable House   35–39
Urban Rural Systems | ur.systems
Location Batam, Indonesia
Completed 2019
Photography Carli Teteris

Mausam—House of the Seasons   40–43
Zero Studio | facebook.com/zerostudioofficial
Location Mannarkand, India
Completed 2017
Photography Ar Hamid MM

FAB House   47–51
TDO | tdoarchitecture.com
Location North Shields, United Kingdom
Completed 2018
Photography Peter Cook

SysHaus   52–61
Arthur Casas | arthurcasas.com
Location São Paulo, Brazil
Completed 2018
Photography Filippo Bamberghi

Đại Kim House   64–67
Aline Architect | aline-design.vn
Location Hanoi, Vietnam
Completed 2018
Photography Triệu Chiến

Double Duplex   68–73
Batay-Csorba Architects | batay-csorba.com
Location Toronto, ON, Canada
Completed 2015
Photography Doublespace Photography

Powerhouse   76–79
Interface Studio Architects (ISA) | is-architects.com
Location Philadelphia, PN, United States
Completed 2016
Photography Sam Oberter

Woodview Mews   80–85
Geraghty Taylor | gth-architects.com
Location London, United Kingdom
Project Lead Brendan Geraghty
Completed 2015
Photography Gareth Gardener

Ross Street House   91–97
Ross Street Design | rossstreetdesign.com
Location Madison, WI, United States
Completed Ongoing
Photography Zane Williams

Campbell Street   103–11
DKO Architecture and SLAB | dko.com.au | slabarchitecture.com
Location Melbourne, VIC, Australia
Completed 2017
Photography Kate Ballis, Tom Blachford

Whittaker Cube   112–17
Dravitzki Brown | dravitzkibrown.co.nz
Location Kakanui, New Zealand
Completed 2016
Photography Alister Brown

3500 Millimetre House   120–25
AGo Architects | agoarchitecture.com
Location South Jakarta, Indonesia
Completed 2018
Photography Kafin Noe'man

Mills House 126–33
Austin Maynard Architects | maynardarchitects.com
Location Melbourne, VIC, Australia
Completed 2016
Photography Peter Bennetts

Surry Hills House 135–42
Benn & Penna Architecture | bennandpenna.com
Location Sydney, NSW, Australia
Completed 2015
Photography Tom Ferguson

Tenhachi House 142–47
Tenhachi Architect & Interior Design | ten-hachi.com
Location Kanagawa, Japan
Completed 2015
Photography Akihide Mishima

Hunter's Point 151–55
Pearl Homes | pearlhomesdevelopments.com
Location Cortez, FL, United States
Completed ongoing
Photography Courtesy of Pearl Homes

Limestone House 156–63
John Wardle Architects | johnwardlearchitects.com
Location Melbourne, VIC, Australia
Completed 2018
Photography 2021 Dianna Snape reproduced with permission from *Architecture—At the heart of the Home* published by Thames & Hudson Australia

Catskills House 167–75
J_spy Architecture | jspyarchitecture.com
Location White Lake, NY, United States
Completed 2017
Photography Amanda Kirkpatrick

Holmberg House 176–81
Estudio Borrachia | estudioborrachia.com
Location Belgrano, Argentina
Completed 2016
Photography Fernando Schapochnik

Living Screen House 185–95
CplusC Architectural Workshop | cplusc.com.au
Location Sydney, NSW, Australia
Completed 2016
Photography Murray Fredericks

BS House 196–203
Reisarchitettura | reisarchitettura.it
Location Ostuni, Puglia, Italy
Completed 2017
Photography Alessandra Bello

Dujardin Mews 209–13
Karakusevic Carson Architects with Maccreanor Lavington Architects | karakusevic-carson.com
Location London, United Kingdom
Completed 2017
Photography Jim Stephenson, Tim Crocker, Emmanuelis Stasaitis

St. Chad's 214–17
Bell Phillips Architects | bellphillips.com
Location Tilbury, United Kingdom
Completed 2017
Photography Kilian O'Sullivan

Hammarby Sjöstad 221–27
White Arkitekter | whitearkitekter.com
Location Stockholm, Sweden
Completed 2018
Photography Åke E:son Lindman, Thomas Zaar

Villa Industria 228–31
Mecanoo | mecanoo.nl
Location Hilversum, The Netherlands
Completed 2018
Photography Courtesy of Mecanoo

Bryant Heights 234–41
Johnston Architects | johnstonarchitects.com
Location Seattle, WA, United States
Completed 2018
Photography Ed Sozinho & Kameron Selby

Marmalade Lane 242–47
Mole Architects | molearchitects.co.uk
Location Cambridge, United Kingdom
Completed 2018
Photography David Butler

Published in Australia in 2022 by
The Images Publishing Group Pty Ltd
ABN 89 059 734 431

OFFICES

Australia
Waterman Business Centre
Suite 64, Level 2 UL40
1341 Dandenong Road
Chadstone, VIC 3148
Tel: +61 3 8564 8122

United States
6 West 18th Street 4B
New York, NY 10011
United States
Tel: +1 212 645 1111

Shanghai
6F, Building C, 838 Guangji Road
Hongkou District, Shanghai 200434
China
Tel: +86 021 31260822

books@imagespublishing.com
www.imagespublishing.com

Copyright © The Images Publishing Group Pty Ltd 2022
The Images Publishing Group Reference Number: 1610

All rights reserved. Apart from any fair dealing for the purposes of private study, research, criticism or review as permitted under the Copyright Act, no part of this publication may be reproduced, stored in a retrieval system or transmitted in any form by any means, electronic, mechanical, photocopying, recording or otherwise, without the written permission of the publisher.

All photography is attributed in the Project Credits on pages 254–55, unless otherwise noted.
Front cover: Filippo Bamberghi (SysHaus, Arthur Casas)

 A catalogue record for this book is available from the National Library of Australia

Title: Future Homes: Sustainable Innovative Designs
Author: Avi Friedman, with Charles Gregoire
ISBN: 9781864709155

This title was commissioned in IMAGES' Melbourne office and produced as follows:
Editorial Georgia (Gina) Tsarouhas, Jeanette Wall, and Kate James *Design and Production* Nicole Boehringer
With thanks to Thais Ometto, Brazil

Printed on 150gsm GalerieArt Matt paper by DZS Grafik (Slovenia)

IMAGES has included on its website a page for special notices in relation to this and its other publications. Please visit www.imagespublishing.com

Every effort has been made to trace the original source of copyright material contained in this book.
The publishers would be pleased to hear from copyright holders to rectify any errors or omissions.
The information and illustrations in this publication have been prepared and supplied by the contributors. While all reasonable efforts have been made to ensure accuracy, the publishers do not, under any circumstances, accept responsibility for errors, omissions and representations express or implied.